"Success is a riddle, and Skip Prichard's business parable shines a light on the answer. By exploring the nine mistakes most leaders and entrepreneurs make, Skip helps us turn desire, gratitude, and belief into powerful tools for achievement."

—**Michael Hyatt**, *USA Today* bestselling author of *Living Forward*

"The essentials of success form the core principles of Skip Prichard's inspiring adventure, THE BOOK OF MISTAKES. Don't miss it!"

—**Ken Blanchard**, coauthor of *The New One Minute Manager*® and *One Minute Mentoring*

"In this engaging story, Skip Prichard gives you a road map of mistakes you can avoid on your life's journey. You'll find yourself in these pages, along with a new way to think about success through curiosity, empathy, and action."

—**Tim Sanders**, author of *Love Is the Killer App: How to Win Business and Influence Friends*

"An inspirational read packed full of wisdom and advice, THE BOOK OF MISTAKES is a MUST-READ for anyone who wants to move forward from the past and create a positive future!"

—**Jon Gordon**, bestselling author of *The Energy Bus* and *The Carpenter*

"Skip Prichard packs a lot of wisdom into this story. Read it to learn the timeless truths of success from a cast of varied characters, and then share the message with others. This truly is a book for readers of all ages."

—**Mark Sanborn**, president of Sanborn & Associates, Inc., author of *The Fred Factor*

"Buy a copy for every graduate in your life before they step into the real world of business. They will thank you for it!"

—**Bob Burg**, coauthor of *The Go-Giver*

"A riveting reminder that while the clues to success are all around us, ultimately the keys are within the person we see in the mirror."

—**Dan Miller**, *New York Times*
bestselling author of *48 Days to the
Work You Love*

"Reminiscent of *The Alchemist*, this book is an operating instruction for life. It should be a mandatory read for people of all ages, especially those getting ready to launch."

—**Lee Woodruff**, *New York Times* bestselling author of *Perfectly
Imperfect*, *In an Instant*, and *Those We Love Most*

"This is no ordinary story. Within these pages, there exists the power to reinvent your life."

—**Andy Andrews**, *New York Times* bestselling
author of *How Do You Kill 11 Million People?*,
The Noticer, and *The Traveler's Gift*

"THE BOOK OF MISTAKES will show you more about success in a few hours than most people come across in decades. Read it, internalize its secrets, and watch your life begin to transform before your eyes."

—**Robert D. Smith**, author of *20,000 Days and Counting*

"If financial success and personal happiness are the Emerald City of Oz, Skip Prichard, in this marvelous book, has paved the perfect Yellow Brick Road to get there. Read it and change your life."

—**Robert Goolrick**, *New York Times* bestselling author of
A Reliable Wife, *Heading Out to Wonderful*,
and *The End of the World as We Know It*

"Skip Prichard's new book is a helpful reminder about the power of the choices we make in life and leadership."

—**Doug Conant**, founder of ConantLeadership and former president and CEO of Campbell Soup Company

"Not only is THE BOOK OF MISTAKES a page-turner that will keep you up at night, it is chock-full of lessons you wish you had learned twenty years ago, and the principles for success that you hope to impart to your children, employees, or coworkers."

—**Ken Abraham**, *New York Times* bestselling author

"An interesting platform for demonstrating the importance of making mistakes and moving forward."

—**Tony Hsieh**, *New York Times* bestselling author of *Delivering Happiness*

"Skip Prichard masterfully tells a story that keeps you interested and engaged throughout the entire book. I highly recommend this book to leaders who aspire to reach their full potential."

—**David M. R. Covey**, coauthor of *Trap Tales: Outsmarting the 7 Hidden Obstacles to Success*

"THE BOOK OF MISTAKES is one book that will set you straight on your path to achieving your goals in record time."

—**John Baldoni**, *Inc.* Top 50 Leadership Expert, executive coach, and author of *Moxie: The Secret to Bold and Gutsy Leadership*

"With a refreshing change of style from traditional personal-development books, Skip's 9 secrets are presented in such an interesting and thought-provoking way that you'll find yourself wanting to highlight, underline, dog-ear pages—anything to ensure that you'll be able to revisit them again and again."

—**Mark Timm**, EVP, Ziglar, Inc.

"THE BOOK OF MISTAKES is an instant classic, a guidebook to achieve success and fulfillment. Read it today and change your tomorrow."

—**Kevin Kruse**, founder and CEO, LEADx,
New York Times bestselling author

"Skip Prichard's new book, THE BOOK OF MISTAKES, is not just another book. This one makes a difference! If you don't read but one book in the coming year, make it this one!"

—**Don Hutson**, coauthor of the *New York Times*
#1 bestselling *The One Minute Entrepreneur*

"Skip Prichard's THE BOOK OF MISTAKES is a compelling narrative and a must-read for anyone who wants to be a better leader and live a life of meaning. If you're in need of a dose of inspiration, you've found it in this book!"

—**Stephen M. R. Covey**, *New York Times* and
#1 *Wall Street Journal* bestselling author of
The Speed of Trust and coauthor of *Smart Trust*

The
BOOK
of
MISTAKES

9 SECRETS TO CREATING A SUCCESSFUL FUTURE

SKIP PRICHARD

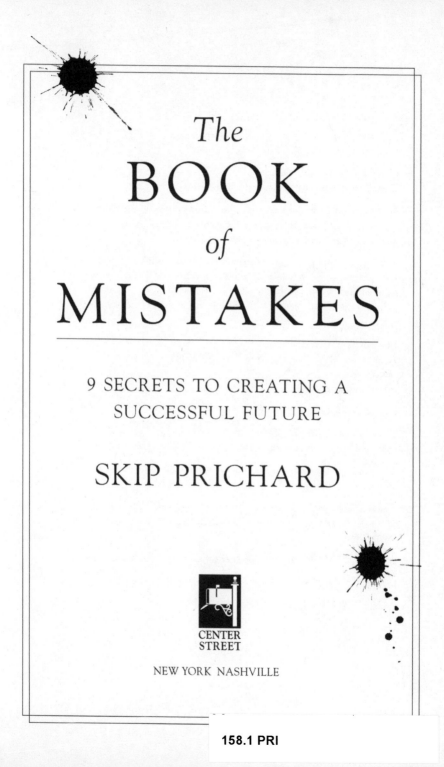

**CENTER
STREET**

NEW YORK NASHVILLE

Center Street
Hachette Book Group
1290 Avenue of the Americas, New York, NY 10104
centerstreet.com
twitter.com/centerstreet

First edition: February 2018

Center Street is a division of Hachette Book Group, Inc. The Center Street name and logo are trademarks of Hachette Book Group, Inc.

The publisher is not responsible for websites (or their content) that are not owned by the publisher.

The Hachette Speakers Bureau provides a wide range of authors for speaking events. To find out more, go to www.HachetteSpeakersBureau.com or call (866) 376-6591.

Library of Congress Cataloging-in-Publication Data has been applied for.

ISBNs: 978-1-4789-7090-3 (hardcover); 978-1-4789-7093-4 (ebook)

Printed in the United States of America

LSC-C

10 9 8 7 6 5 4 3

CONTENTS

PREFACE

My childhood was anything but normal. I suppose that's what most of us think, but we don't realize it until we are fully grown. In my case, I realized it when I was very young, one of six children: four girls, two boys. My parents wanted to make the world a better place and almost left for a Third World country to do mission work. But, instead of moving to the mission, they decided to move the mission to them. Our home would be a place to welcome anyone in need.

How these needy people found us remains a mystery to me, but they came. All types of people walked through the door, making our home a mini United Nations. You were welcome no matter your race or background. Some would stay for a few nights, needing meals and a place to sleep; then they would continue on their life's journey. Others would stay for years, becoming like family members with all of the rights and responsibilities you would expect.

Looking back, the only common trait these people really had was that they were in trouble of some sort: drugs, abuse, unemployment, physical disability, or mental illness. You name it; the litany of problems went on and on. Counseling may not have been of the approved, professional variety, but it was plentiful. A talk with my mom was balm to the soul. Watching both as an observer and a participant in this experiment, I learned so much about people and perspective.

The Riddle

During these years, I began to study what I thought of as a riddle, a puzzle, a question with implications spanning philosophy to psychology. Why did two people with similar challenges end up with such dramatically different results? Why would one go on to secure an education and a good job while another was unable to pry off the deadly grip of addiction's claws?

I remember learning some powerful lessons from the most unexpected people. You wouldn't think to ask an unemployed drug addict about success, but it can be an extraordinary opportunity. When I was sixteen or seventeen, a homeless man shared with me his mistakes and how and why he'd messed up his life. I still recall the conversation and my own resolve not to make the same mistakes he did.

Ask. Seek. Knock.

As the years passed in my life, I read everything I could about success, leadership, and personal development. I studied what many call the "secrets of success." I discovered that they are available to anyone who pursues them. You may have heard the wisdom from the Bible saying, "Ask, and it will be given to you; seek, and you will find; knock, and it will be opened to you." It was the business philosopher Jim Rohn who first taught me that this wisdom was *not* available to all, but only to those who *ask*, those who *seek*, and those who *knock*. Each requires action. When I heard Jim's teaching, I resolved to become an asker, a seeker, and a knocker.

In my pursuit of success, I realized that true success was not about acquiring material possessions or a large income, though these often come as a byproduct of it. And I learned that each and every person in our lives offers wisdom. If you wait for the rich, the powerful, the super-successful to give you a guidebook, you may find yourself waiting for a train that never arrives. The lessons are all around us. The lessons are found in the collective wisdom of those we meet, in the books we read, in the experiences uniquely given to us.

The lessons of success are disguised. They are revealed only to those with a willing, seeking mindset. The questions I most often ask are:

- What was your biggest mistake?
- What would you do over again?
- What made you successful?
- How did you do it?
- What went wrong?

I have learned that we can draw extraordinary lessons from the ordinary people in our lives.

As my own career advanced, I became a CEO myself, successful by many definitions. I still continued to interview people, to ask questions, and to seek wisdom. My job and my travels expose me to a broad group of interesting people. I am blessed and honored to meet and interview business leaders, famous journalists, rock stars, politicians, bestselling authors, the world's greatest sports legends, and many celebrities. What I have learned is that many of them are successful because they overcame hardships and their own doubts and developed a resolve to succeed.

This book is a fable of a young man and a young woman in a mysterious journey to learn the nine mistakes that trip up many. By avoiding these nine mistakes, most of us can change our lives for the better. Wherever you are on your own life's journey, whether starting out or well down the road, you are here for a purpose. And that purpose is still achievable, no matter your age or condition.

In order to fulfill your dreams, it is imperative to become an asker, a seeker, and a knocker. That's where the magic starts. That's where the riddle of success is answered.

Ask. Seek. Knock.

The door is in front of you.

PROLOGUE

He pushed forward, the passage narrowing and darkening. His lungs burned as he began the ascent up the stairs. Each step echoed off the stone walls, and he slowed his climb so as not to alert anyone to his presence, not that anyone would be awake.

His temples throbbed and pulsed in rhythm with the beat in his imagination, conjuring up the chants of morning prayers and distracting him from the pain in his legs and shoulders. He switched the leather satchel from one arm to the other and faced the wooden door. Barely seeing in the dim light, he pushed open the door. Its hinges squealed, yielding to his pressure.

Once inside, he moved immediately to the cathedral's nave and crossed into the north transept. He could traverse the abbey blindfolded by now. He gently laid the satchel at his feet and felt for the loose stone in the wall. Ever mindful of the risk he was taking, he worked the stone from its resting place.

This mission he was on originated directly from the Prior, and it was as mysterious as the man himself. He didn't question. His job was to follow orders, dutifully fulfilling his vows. The last years he had spent carefully scribing ten copies of an ancient book of wisdom from the desert lands of the far south, the lands of man-made stone mountains that reached to the sky. No one else was permitted to read its words. Now, for reasons unknown to him, he was to take a single manuscript and hide it behind the stone wall. He was to do this each night until all ten copies, one for each of the nine Teachers and one for the new Keeper, were distributed. Each night, he had noticed that the hollowed space was empty. He knew the Prior did not want the risk of having all the manuscripts in one place at one time, so he followed, with precision, the plan outlined for him.

Tonight was the final night.

He pushed the manuscript deep inside the wall and replaced the stone.

He sensed something. He knew these walls. The presence of something sinister threatened the stillness. He could feel it, though he couldn't see it.

A loud crash echoed behind him, coming from the presbytery.

He stopped breathing. He crept on his hands and knees, painfully, willing himself out of sight. He had been told that someone might try to steal the book, though, admittedly, he paid little mind to the warning. After all, no one had bothered him during the whole time he worked on each manuscript.

The book increased the odds of success for all those who applied its wisdom. Not having to fall into the common traps of mankind, it became possible to accomplish plans at great speed. This was true for individuals, and even more so for a group of committed practitioners. No one wanted the book to fall into the wrong hands.

Row after row, he worked his way to the entrance to the vestry. He was patient. Any time now.

And then it was time. His brothers would soon be filing in for Nocturnus, the first service of the new day, three o'clock in what most considered the dead of night.

He was silent, waiting as he had been instructed, patiently planning to slip into line when they arrived.

His unknown enemy realized what was happening, too, and called out, "I know you're here! Give it to me. You have no need for it. I will gladly pay you any sum you ask!"

The monk silently laughed to himself. *What need have I of money?* he thought, recalling his vow of poverty.

And then the thief was there, right in front of the monk, so close he could feel the stench of his breath, the odor of his body. His hands were on his neck, and he gasped for breath. The man's fingers dug into his flesh, tearing, insisting. "You *will* give it to me, or you will die…"

But, at that moment, the man dropped to the floor. The monk gulped in air and looked up to see what had saved him. In the darkness, the body of his attacker was lifted up onto strong shoulders and then carried off. He heard the door.

He knew what had happened.

The Keeper had been here all along, protecting the book and protecting him.

The monk smiled, even as his heart still pounded, knowing that the book remained safe.

He wondered how long it would remain a secret. *When will the entire world be ready for its wisdom? Will there be a day when the darker forces are so diminished that it will be freely available to all?*

At that moment, his brothers arrived. With a knowing nod to the Prior, he took his place in line.

Last night, he had burned the original manuscript, just as he had been instructed. The ancient language was now long forgotten, with only a few who had the ability to translate it properly. Still, he had followed his instructions to the letter.

He could finally relax. The book was safely out of the monastery. Its secrets were protected for another generation.

DAVID

The alarm went off at precisely 5:30. It was Thursday. The weekend was in sight, but the week's responsibilities felt less than halfway done. The thoughts of work were stabbing into David's mind, surgically waking him even as he tried to push them away.

Shifting in bed, David reached over, hit snooze, and tried to enjoy another ten minutes of sleep. When the annoying sound blared through his apartment's bedroom again, he reluctantly pushed himself out of bed and shambled into the bathroom. Looking in the mirror, he did a double take.

His hair had morphed into something way beyond typical bed head, swooping up and to the left in such a dramatic way that it made him smile. Though he was quite clearly no longer a teenager, he saw glimmers of his younger self. His brown eyes retained their mixture of wonder and amusement. Most would describe him as handsome, though he knew he wasn't headed for the big screen anytime soon.

Turning the shower to its hottest setting, he mentally coaxed the water to heat up, knowing that was unlikely in his aging apartment building. About fifteen minutes later, he was in the kitchen, making coffee and scrolling through his e-mail.

Worry was working on him earlier in the day than usual. When had it started? David remembered how carefree he'd felt when he graduated from college and took his current job, almost two years ago. Moving into his own place was almost anticlimactic. No big deal, nothing special. It felt right. At the beginning, he would have described himself as neither overly confident nor nervous, just ready for what would come next.

Somewhere in the last year, things had shifted, and not exactly for the better. His paychecks weren't coming fast enough. Unpaid bills were piling up on the table. Those two credit cards, originally for convenience, now had growing balances. It's funny, he thought, when he took the job and signed the lease, he never imagined that it would be anything other than easy. He hadn't spent as much time developing a budget as he should have. Truth be told, he really hadn't spent *any* time developing a budget. He hadn't even thought about utilities, and he had definitely miscalculated the tax bite from his pay.

And then there was his job. It had started out well. His boss liked him, took him under his wing, and acted more like an older brother or mentor rather than a superior. That lulled him into a false sense of security. Three months in and his boss was off to join a new start-up, leaving David reporting to someone new who wasn't invested in him and who didn't laugh at his jokes.

That was fine enough until he messed up. It was really nothing, at least to him. But his new boss acted as if it was a blot on his record that would never be erased. He couldn't believe it mattered that much. After all, he had only forgotten to call back a customer. The company wasn't in danger.

Two weeks ago, he finally learned what was really up. He never thought a small office could be so political, nor that someone would be so underhanded. Someone had clearly set him up for a fall. It wasn't really the customer call. It was more. He was blamed for a raft of things he didn't do, most of them stemming from rumors that seemed to originate directly with the boss.

It wasn't supposed to be this way. He thought of one of his friends, who'd graduated just a few years before him. Quick promotions. Big money. His name regularly in the news. At first, David was genuinely happy for him. But as he toiled on in what seemed like a meaningless job and struggled with the bills, he found it difficult to stomach his friend's success. And then he hated himself for thinking that way.

Scrolling through his e-mail, he saw an unexpected, terse message from his boss. He read it again and again in an attempt to interpret the meaning behind the words.

I need to see you in my office at 11:00.

That was it. No explanation.

He felt his pulse quicken, and he sucked in a breath. His eyes involuntarily closed and he massaged his temples, willing it all to go away.

Looking back at his messages, he saw another one. This one was a cheery note from Mom. He put his phone down and took another sip of coffee.

His parents had no idea what it was like. They were proud of their college graduate who was gainfully employed at a good company. They had bragged about his accomplishments, embarrassing him a bit, within their circle of friends. He hadn't shared that his doting boss was gone, how his new boss had him unfairly under the microscope, or that he was struggling. He didn't share that he felt his job was meaningless, the daily repetition boring him to tears as he slogged through one e-mail after another. Answering these e-mails drained him, though he was required to respond within a day at most. Often he found himself imagining a different life, one where he wasn't imprisoned in a dull gray cubicle.

He hadn't shared the stress, the bills, nor the anxiousness with anyone. Why would he add to their worries? Dad was already stressed out enough over how the stock market decline was eating into his retirement. And Mom's ongoing health challenges made sharing troubling news unwise, or at least unwelcome. About the only thing they were expecting to hear from him was that he had found "the one" and that a wedding and kids were inevitable. He avoided that question, too, staying vague about his dating so as not to encourage his mother's hopes for an immediate end to his bachelorhood.

"Will I actually be fired? For stuff I had nothing to do with?" he wondered aloud, his voice cutting through the relative silence of the morning. The only answer was from the heating system, which kicked on at that very moment with a roar.

Maybe the meeting wasn't about his job. Maybe it was a new assignment or something completely different. Maybe his boss was going to apologize for blaming him unfairly.

He decided to scan the local news to take his mind somewhere else. One of the city's prominent business leaders was making headlines for some charitable work, a warm story of giving back to the community. He read about a new play debuting in town and about the hockey team's trade of a star player. The coach was interviewed about the prospects for a big season.

The news didn't calm him much. David exhaled, silently willing his stress to fade with his breath. He put his cup in the sink, grabbed his computer bag, and left for his walk to work. This tension was all too much, he thought, wondering how in the world life had grown so complex so quickly.

It was an unusually cold autumn day, with winds that plucked the leaves off the trees and sent them into a spinning, colorful show before pulling them high into the air and then dropping them scattershot across the lawn. Passing the corner church, the one with the stained glass windows and the heavy wooden door, he noticed a man slumped over against the opposite wall. A crude cardboard sign told a lifetime's story in a few sentences. David actually imagined, for the briefest of moments, that he might become homeless himself. It was as if his mind raced to the most negative possibilities of getting fired and then evicted. He shook his head, hard, as if he could knock the thought right out of his head. He wasn't even close to that situation at this point, and he could always return home. This stress was getting to him.

At the same time, something else tugged at him: The hopeful thoughts of that teenager he once was. The thoughts of moving up the corporate ladder, making good money, hosting parties, enjoying his wife and kids. How everything would work out for good—thoughts that flashed brightly and then seemed to disappear.

When had those thoughts been replaced by thoughts of survival? Of getting fired? Of the completely irrational—like such fears as being homeless?

Glancing ahead at the busy street, he decided to take the shortcut through the park. He was a creature of habit and generally oblivious. He didn't notice the people around him. He didn't notice much of anything. Instead, he purposely picked up speed to make it in to work and begin another day handling problems, shuffling paper, and grinding through a slog of e-mail.

Lost in thought, David almost tripped over a young woman who was frantically grabbing faded yellow papers that the wind had pulled out of her hands. Despite the fact she was not winning the war against the wind, she was laughing and obviously having a great time, as if she had planned this little game all along. David quickly began snatching the pages out of the air with such speed and ease that she stepped back and admired his skill.

"Thank you. I would never have been able to do that."

David nodded, bowed slightly at his waist, and said, "At your service." Handing the pages back to her, he politely smiled and kept going.

Minutes later, he was standing in front of his office building. He glanced at his watch and realized he was early. Extremely early. He decided to waste a little time, and so he passed his office building and entered the corner shop. Having had his fill of coffee, he perused the long list of teas. Finally settling on a robust black tea mixed with a fruit flavor, he angled to a far table where he resolved to calm his thoughts and settle down before work.

As the sounds of the hungry morning commuters surrounded him, he steeled himself for the day ahead. Leaving the shop, he approached the revolving door to his office building. As he pushed his way into the lobby, he felt the transformation begin. Inside the office, he felt different, as if cloaked in a costume, a minor character in a play. He nodded to a few coworkers and made his way to his desk.

A few hours later, it was time to meet with the boss. David walked slowly down the hallway, his palms sweaty, his face flushed.

Trying to be confident, he managed a weak smile as he stepped to the open office door.

The meeting was over in two minutes.

He wasn't fired, but he was given a verbal warning. There was little room left for error.

David surprised his manager by not arguing. He even surprised himself when he heard his own voice promise to turn things around. Immediately after exiting the office, he headed for the bathroom and splashed water on his face to cool down. He wondered if he had sounded as pathetic as he felt. He couldn't lose this job, not now, not with no savings. His family, his friends, everyone thought he was hitting it out of the park.

If he were fired, it would be a shock to them. At home, he was always confident, had lettered in two sports in high school, played in college, exceptional grades, two sterling internships. He was well liked, and everyone imagined that he was on the fast track to a highly successful career.

He couldn't fail. He would not fail.

David knew that something had to change, but he didn't know where to begin.

That evening as he started back through the park, he heard a rustling sound. Looking up, he saw a piece of paper that had lodged neatly under a rock. Its color was the same faded yellow he remembered from that morning. He walked over and picked it up before glancing around as if the woman would still be nearby. Tucking the yellow paper in his jacket pocket, he continued walking home, thinking he might run into the young woman again the next morning. He smiled as he remembered their brief meeting, her contagious laughter, the twinkle in her eyes.

At home, he hung up his jacket and then reached into the pocket. On the folded paper was a note:

NORTH CAFÉ 10:00 a.m. Friday, September 14.

Flipping over the fold, he read:

Your success is only possible if you avoid the nine mistakes. Most people never realize these until it's too late. Don't let that happen. Meet me in the last booth by the windows. They'll know you're coming.

It was signed with the name of the man who had been in the paper that morning for his charitable work.

This must have been hers, David thought, his mind conjuring up the image of her attractive face and the sound of her contagious laugh. *I wonder if I could just sit in. Maybe I'll go and say I found the paper and then see what happens. This is just what I need!*

His thoughts drifted off to what he had heard about the man who was a benefactor to many: his successes, his work in the city, and his connections. *He could be a way out for me,* thought David. *Maybe I could work for him or network into a new position. I'm definitely going to this meeting.*

That night, as he stared at the ceiling over his bed, listening to the sounds of the traffic, he mulled the day's events over and over again. He replayed the conversation with his boss. As he thought about it, he remembered sounding more confident. He wondered whether his mind was subtly changing the actual tone of the meeting to make himself feel better.

He whispered a prayer, more a plea or a wish, that this all would change. He didn't just want to get things on track at work and pay down his bills. He wanted his confidence back. He wanted his dreams back!

"I wish I could sense when I was about to slip and make major mistakes. Or erase them completely."

Just for effect, he fist-punched the air above him.

He smiled and finally fell into a deep sleep, the best sleep he had had in a long time.

THE BEGINNING

David arrived at the North Café early enough to intercept the woman, explain, and then be on his way if things seemed too... strange. She wasn't there, so he asked to be seated in the last booth by the windows.

He glanced up at the clock. Less than two minutes later, he did it again. He was sitting in the last booth, his leg jumping as if it were on batteries. His server was faithfully refilling coffee while someone out of sight was steadily mopping the floor, cleaning the morning rush away.

Exactly four minutes and one cup of coffee later, he glanced up to see an elderly man walk in, glance about the small room, and look right at him. Even with the dishes clanking in the kitchen and the sloshing noise from the nearby mop, David could hear the man faintly whistling as he walked toward him.

David glanced up at the clock again to note that the host was right on time. As expected. But this pillar of the community was not at all what he expected.

David knew this man was one of the most successful of his generation. He owned large tracts of property and had long ago sold several businesses that started locally but quickly expanded around the world. His mind's eye had painted a vivid picture of a man dressed impeccably, shoes shined brightly, trousers neatly pressed, with a small handkerchief peeking out of a tailored sport coat.

Instead, the Old Man was dressed casually in faded jeans and worn loafers, with an unshaven face and a nondescript shirt. The only thing that hinted at his wealth was his watch, though David was unable to discern the make and model with only a furtive glance as the man took the seat opposite him.

The Old Man smiled and looked across the table with piercing eyes that seemed to probe deep, searching, not judging, but evaluating, as if with a look he could conduct due diligence and know everything there was to know. It was a look David didn't expect and, catching him off guard, David moved his own gaze elsewhere, shifting in his seat. Perhaps there was something to this more interesting than money.

"I'm so glad to meet you and am so glad you are here this morning. I knew you would come," the Old Man began with a smile that was bright and genuine.

David found himself under the seemingly all-seeing gaze in the Old Man's booth. There was still no sign of the beautiful young lady from the park. All of the lines he had rehearsed to explain his presence were useless now.

The Old Man, now comfortably in his seat, looked back across the table and repeated himself. "Yes, indeed, I knew you would come."

"Uh, sorry?" David said, adding, "I think you may be mistaken. You see, I . . . I . . . I was helping someone who dropped some papers and I . . . I . . ." He trailed off, not knowing exactly what to say next and thinking that he sounded two steps from a mental health facility.

"Young man, everything happens for a reason. And I am glad that you found the invitation and made it here today. It was for you."

"Invitation? Me? No, I just found it, and I was curious. About the nine mistakes?"

"Yes, but you cannot possibly understand that right now. Don't rush right into it. There will be time."

The server appeared at the table, and the Old Man grasped his hand warmly and smiled. They were apparently close friends.

"The usual?" the server asked, filling up a coffee cup and nodding back to someone behind the counter.

"You know me too well. And what would you like?" the Old Man asked David as he rummaged through the bag at his side.

"I'll take the Continental," David said, after admiring the menu's description.

David looked across the table at this successful man who didn't seem surprised at his presence and was acting not only as if this was normal but also as if it was completely expected. At the very least, he figured, he would have a nice breakfast and say he had met the Old Man. His family would want to know all about it, and he already was wondering how he would explain it. But David realized he needed more from this chance encounter. He needed answers, a way out of the trap of his life. He needed a direction, almost any direction, just a bit of guidance to lift him out of the heaviness that surrounded him lately.

The Old Man pulled out a small leather book. It was obviously old. In fact, it was so weathered David wouldn't have been surprised if it was at least one hundred years old. The Old Man caressed it, then, holding it to his chest, smiled as if he were holding a grandchild and showering the kid with love. He pulled reading glasses from his pocket, then flipped open the first page.

"Ah, forgive me. I get excited every time I have the chance to share this. It is very special to me. But before I do, tell me all about you."

David was normally somewhat reserved with strangers. He would usually start with his job title, his company, and maybe throw in where he went to college. For some reason, that all seemed so trivial in the presence of the Old Man. So he started in a different place. He began telling the Old Man about where he grew up, how he grew up, his siblings, his parents, his dreams, his hopes. The Old Man listened intently and sincerely, asking questions, genuinely wanting to know more.

At one point, the Old Man interrupted, sensing something. "I need to ask you. What are you so afraid of?"

The question felt like a boxer's unexpected knockout punch. David felt his throat constrict. He tried to talk, but it felt like he was choking, so he took a drink of water and tried to regain his composure. He was trying so desperately to be honest, but with a positive spin on everything. After all, he was hoping to impress the Old Man and gain a powerful ally. Internally, he was in turmoil. He just didn't want to admit what was really going on in his life.

It seemed like minutes were going by, but the Old Man said nothing and acted completely at ease with the silence that had settled between them. It was like he knew that David was trying to formulate the right words.

Finally, David relented, though he felt like the umpire had already called him out and declared this battle lost. He decided to share more of the story. It was difficult to start, but, once he did, he felt the freedom to express his deepest thoughts. It was like a dam that, unable to hold the raging waters back a moment longer, had finally broken: his mother's health challenges, the expectations of his family, his unfair boss and the frightening warning, the struggles at work, the bills piled on the counter, numbers glaring at him ominously in red ink, the expectations he had for himself, how he wanted to perform well, and how he just couldn't disappoint his family.

All of it, now out, hanging in the air. With each revelation, David felt a weight lifting off of himself. For better or worse, he couldn't stop sharing.

The Old Man listened intently. He asked a few more questions. None of it seemed to surprise him. "Thank you," said the Old Man. "I know where you are. I have walked the path you are on." The Old Man's head was nodding ever so slightly. His probing eyes left for just a second, drifting somewhere else. "Tell me more." And with that, David continued his story.

Before David realized it, the server had cleared the dishes from the table, and the Old Man had paid the check. David had mindlessly been eating while talking and, switching from his fears, David shared some of his deepest hopes for the future. Though the details of where he wanted his personal and professional life seemed clear to him as he spoke, he realized that the specifics weren't important. All he really wanted was to feel in control, fulfilling his purpose, and making a real difference.

The Old Man sat back in the booth, took a deep breath, and smiled in a way that warmed the room, the skin around his eyes crinkling slightly at the edges. "Do you think you are ready?"

"I guess so. Maybe I need a notepad."

"Not that kind of ready. The beginning is when you have more questions than answers. Readiness is when your desire is stronger than your distraction."

David smiled and replied, "I don't know if all of that is true, but you have my attention. What do you think?"

In a more serious tone, the Old Man continued, "I believe you are in a perfect state of mind to learn these lessons. If you really are committed to this process, I believe it will transform your thinking—and your life. Well, what do you say?"

David didn't quite know how to respond. He wasn't sure where this was going, and his mind began to wonder again what he was doing here and why he had shared all of this personal information.

"Well, say yes or no. And I hope you say yes."

"What am I saying yes to, exactly?" David said, his left eye squinting.

"To studying the nine mistakes," the Old Man said in an almost bewildered, slightly chiding tone, as if David was completely and utterly lost. "If you want the things you say you do, you need to learn these mistakes. If you're looking to escape your current situation, I know of no other way."

"I've enjoyed this time with you. I appreciate you listening to my hopes and my problems, though I'm still somewhat confused about how and why you expected me. I feel like maybe I hit my head and this isn't real. But I am curious. Yes, I would very much like to know the nine mistakes. Actually, I feel like I need to know them. What are they?"

The Old Man laughed. Not a casual laugh, but a deep belly laugh that reverberated throughout the corner of the café and surrounded them. It was warm, sincere, and infectious. Before he realized it, David was also laughing. And it felt good.

"Why are we laughing?" David managed to get out as the infectious laughter continued, releasing built up emotion.

"Do you think I can just hand them over to you? I suppose I could." The Old Man's hands brushed his whiskers, then moved to caress the book. "But the power wouldn't be there. I'm not sure it would even work." His eyes moved to the book, and he seemed lost in a distant thought. "It's funny, there have been people trying to steal this book for hundreds of years. They think to possess the book itself is to have its power, or perhaps that the secrets are just in the words on the page. That isn't the case at all. Still others specialize in criticism over creation. Whenever there is positive power, you will find naysayers and hope squelchers that want to destroy someone else's dreams. And so each generation must find a way to keep the wisdom safe and the dreams within our hearts protected."

The server appeared, gave a knowing half smile, and filled the Old Man's coffee cup one final time. The Old Man looked down at his cup, which was practically overflowing.

"This cup is full and so are you. Before you can absorb each lesson, you need to have room in your cup. You need to absorb each one," the Old Man said, as he swallowed down a large gulp of steaming java. "So we need to share each lesson in a way that you can get it."

Compared with David's sharing of his life's dreams throughout the meal, the Old Man hadn't really said that much, but now he was fully engaged and ready to talk. "Knowledge arrives in loud bursts, but wisdom only speaks in silence. Acceptance of the new is possible only with space from the old. If you don't take time to discard the unnecessary, you will have no room for what matters."

Then, reflecting quietly, the Old Man nodded almost imperceptibly, as if agreeing with an internal voice. "If you are committed to learning them, then we will teach them to you."

"We?"

"Yes, we. I'm not exactly the best person to teach them."

"When do we begin?" David asked. He heard one voice asking the Old Man about when to begin and what to expect while also hearing an internal voice asking if he was insane, if he knew what he was doing, and how he would explain this to anyone.

"Often we are on a path before our conscious minds realize it. We have already begun," the Old Man said. He was putting on his coat and already shuffling to the door.

"Wait, you don't even have my number!" David said, following him, curious and insistent.

"You have no idea the journey you are about to take. Now that it has started, almost nothing can stop it. In fact, the teachers will appear at just the right time and in the most unlikely and unusual places. I wish I could be there myself. You'll have a rendezvous soon!"

And with that, the Old Man seemed to vanish along the busy street, leaving David standing awkwardly in the doorway. David put on his own jacket and glanced up and down the street, but didn't see him anywhere.

Somehow David must have missed the Old Man slipping a piece of weathered paper into his hands. He looked at the writing, and, after reading it, carefully tucked the message into his pocket.

THE BEGINNING

The beginning is when you have more questions than
answers.

Readiness is when your desire is stronger than your
distraction.

Knowledge comes in bursts, but wisdom speaks in silence.

Acceptance of the new is possible only with space from the
old.

Discard the unnecessary to make room for what matters.

Often we are on a journey long before our conscious minds
realize it.

ARIA

⌘⌘⌘

AMERICAN COLONIES, 1771

Every muscle in her body coiled tightly in expectation. She felt the perspiration beading on her forehead, trickling down the side of her face. The air was electric with anticipation. Perched on a wooden ladder in her uncle Raymond's study, Aria balanced the candle in one hand while maintaining a shaky grip. The beat of horses' hooves approached. Came to a halt outside. There was no more time.

It was where he said it would be, but it was just out of reach.

She pushed some books aside to set the candle down. Careful to keep her skirts out of the way, she stepped up to the top rung, gripping the edge of a shelf to keep a precarious balance with one hand as she stretched the other to tug at the large black box. The ladder swayed, and she steadied herself, taking in a sharp breath while listening intently.

And then she had it; tucking the box awkwardly under her arm so she could hold the candle, she was down the ladder and across the room. She knew her uncle would not last the night. She wondered if she would, either.

She pulled the box to her chest, its contents secure. Risking a quick peek, she lifted the lid and saw the yellowed papers. There it was—the manuscript that was now unexpectedly toying with her, dragging her from her quiet life into the unknown danger of what seemed a foolhardy mission.

Her sense of duty pulsed through her being. If the manuscript fell into the wrong hands, she would never forgive herself. Her uncle had warned her there were men who had come here for it. They weren't the first to think the book could give them power over others, as if it were some mystical thing. Aria smirked in spite of the situation, thinking how wrong they were. Still, the wisdom in these pages could be used for evil purposes, and those who would steal it rather than inherit it could do a great deal of harm with its lessons. Her uncle had kept its secrets safe since long before he became her protector, when he took her in as his ward all those years ago. She longed to please him until he drew his last breath. Even if she didn't fully understand all the pieces of the game, the why behind it all, she gritted her teeth in determination to accomplish what he asked.

Her heart was beating fast as she made her way out of the study. If they caught her now, it was all over.

Her uncle's words were with her, pushing her on. She knew what was at stake.

She stopped suddenly, something catching her attention mid-stride. She blew out the candle and listened to the wind rattling the shutters outside. No voices. The silence was suspicious.

Were they in the house?

Like a deer, she moved gracefully and silently down the hall to the back parlor. The moon shone brightly through the windows. The fireplace was still warm, golden embers smoldering with the occasional flicker of flame.

Yes. They were in the house. She could feel someone. Or something. A presence heavier than any she had known.

A thud and a voice, calling out in pain, confirmed it. Someone had tripped somewhere in the dark in another room. Thankful that Uncle Raymond's home was one of the largest in the area, she maneuvered herself to look carefully down the hall. Aria glanced to the far door and then to the fire and back again. She could see no one.

Aria studied the door to the parlor as she took a few calming breaths. Her senses were on high alert. She hadn't felt this energized in months. She carefully removed the papers from the box and examined them, making sure they were all there, before returning them to the safety of the box.

A thought crossed her mind. Her eighteenth birthday was coming up. She wondered if she would make it. Only a week ago, she had calculated how old she would be when the century turned; 1800 sounded like forever away. Now, with the manuscript clutched to her chest, her next birthday seemed just as far away.

She stole a glance through the windows. More men had arrived.

Aria willed the thoughts out of her mind and tried to focus. She weighed the decision, wishing she had more time to think of an alternative. Her uncle wouldn't need to know if she failed. He could die thinking she had succeeded.

But no, she knew what had to be done, and so she pushed out the doubts and focused once again on accomplishing her mission.

Crouching by the fireplace, Aria wrapped a cloth around her

left hand once, twice, three times before tying it around her arm. She looked around the room. Tears unexpectedly welled up from deep within her being, falling onto her cheeks and momentarily blurring her vision. All her most precious memories had happened within these walls. Though she could wipe the tears away, she couldn't wipe away the emotion. The line between the past and the future taunted and teased. She knew she was about to cross the threshold of that line, leaving behind the safety of one life for the unknown of another.

She picked up the broom from the side of the fireplace, took a final deep breath, and then thrust the end of the straw into the fire. Almost immediately the fire roared with approval, sending flames high into the air, lighting the broom end. Aria ran to the curtains and lit them on fire before racing to the next room and tossing the burning broom onto Uncle Raymond's favorite chair, the one where she had so often sat on his lap and heard stories of faraway places. She remembered how much he enjoyed putting on a show for his guests from the comfort of this chair. Even the servants would linger from their duties to listen.

Aria was glad that the servants weren't here now to see what she was doing. They would never understand.

The fire was now raging, and she heard a shout from outside. More men would be inside in minutes and surely heading right for her and the brightness, the conflagration lighting the night.

She picked up the box and slipped back down the hallway. Seeing no one, she paused when she heard a sound. A second later, she hid behind the large draperies of the room nearest the door. She knew she couldn't linger long or she would never make it out alive. She was trying not to cough from the wisps of smoke and the dust stirred up by her unexpected visit. She couldn't see anything and held herself motionless. If she was breathing, she didn't know, so still was she as she listened for the sounds of intruders.

And then she knew that the sound she had heard was the house itself. It was as if it were alive and moaning, knowing that its existence was threatened. She felt guilty, knowing that she was the cause.

She risked peeking back out and spotted a man limping, but still moving quickly toward the fire. Knowing she didn't have much time, Aria waited a few more seconds and then slipped out from behind the curtains. She headed in the opposite direction. In a moment, she was exiting the back door. She felt a tug on her sleeve, pulling her back, and she realized her clothing had caught on a nail outside by the door. She imagined it was the house, reaching out and making one last plea for her to undo the damage she had started. She tore free, and the night enveloped her, its blackness a welcome cover, the sweet, clean air filling her lungs. She moved with ease, knowing every inch of the property surrounding the home she had grown up in. At the top of the hill, she slipped behind the large boulder where she had loved to hide from the world to sit and read.

The windows were lit up; the fire raged. The light gave her glimpses of shadows, of men fleeing outside. As far as she could tell, no one knew of her presence, nor was anyone looking for her. She took a deep breath and released the tension she had been holding inside.

How she had remained undiscovered was a mystery, an answer to a prayer. She turned back to leave. Her ears caught a faint sound on the wind, lifted up from below.

That voice!

Aria stopped herself midturn and spun back toward the house. She couldn't believe it. Her mind struggled to make the impossible possible, to make some sense of it, to explain his presence in the night at her home.

Not possible.

She squinted, certain her eyes were playing tricks on her, but her squint only solidified the certainty. It was him. Alexander. He was talking to another man who was much older, with white hair and a face not soon forgotten, with pockmarked skin, sunken cheekbones, and a sour mouth that matched his angry visage. The contrast between this man and Alexander was stark.

What was Alexander doing here?

Aria watched him from afar, knowing that no one would see her perched so high above the home. She strained to hear, but she couldn't make out any words. Her eyes saw Alexander, but her mind's eye took her to her intended destination. She pictured her uncle, in bed and asking for her. *How I hope he is still among the living,* she thought. When her uncle took ill at his friend Robert's house, she had insisted on taking him home, but they would hear none of it. They immediately prepared a room for him and called a doctor, who agreed he should stay right where he was. There was no way of knowing that his condition would worsen and worsen; each day the hope of a recovery seemed to dim with the life inside. Her uncle was beloved by everyone he met and so a stream of well-wishers attempted to gain access to him, only to be turned away by Robert's wife, Mae, who was ferociously protective.

Aria's mind refocused when the man with Alexander went one direction and he another. Then Alexander stopped at the back door. His hands began to fumble with something. Aria looked down at her ripped sleeve and realized what drew his attention. He had spotted some thread from where her clothing had torn on the nail. She knew she couldn't possibly be seen from where he was, but still, she squatted lower. Alexander's eyes swept the back of the home and then upward. She held her breath. A large crack split the air as the top of the home lit up the darkness. Flames licked the outside walls. It seemed that the entire house was now engulfed in a raging inferno. She looked back and saw Alexander disappear around the side of the house.

Realizing she had her hand on her beating heart, she steadied herself. Her other hand clutched the box she hoped those men believed was lost in the flames. What was Alexander doing with them? Was he involved in the plot to steal the book? What other explanation could there be?

Exhausted, Aria could see the earliest glimmer of dawn as she took a final gaze at the home that she loved. Memories, one by one, flooded back. She was only six when the accident claimed the lives of her parents and her uncle took her in. They had been nearly inseparable ever since. This home was the only one she had really ever known.

She pushed the thoughts out of her mind. The present was what mattered now. She must start moving.

She unwrapped her hand, wiped the tears from her eyes, and carefully made her way through the winding path of the woods. It would take her an hour before she would be back with her uncle. She whispered a prayer for his recovery and hoped, above all, that she would have the opportunity to see him again.

⌘ ⌘ ⌘

MISTAKE ONE

Several days had passed with no word from the Old Man. As he walked to work, David found himself walking more slowly, noticing more, and looking for the young woman who had started it all when her papers went flying. He dropped by the café, too, in hopes of finding the Old Man there.

All of his worries seemed insignificant now that he had met the Old Man. He wanted to know the nine mistakes. He wondered what they were, where they came from, why it would matter. He tried to put it all out of his mind. He tried to concentrate on his job. Getting his boss to like him, or at least not have it in for him, was also rattling around in the back of his head.

Still, the Old Man's words seemed to cling to him, never letting his mind wander far.

"I guess mistake number one is obsessing over nothing!" he said aloud before looking around to see if anyone heard him. Muttering under his breath, he added, "Or it may be going crazy after learning about these mistakes."

One afternoon, David was returning to work from lunch. After pushing the button for the elevator, he caught a sideways glimpse of himself in a reflection off the gold elevator doors. He noticed he was slouching and straightened up, hearing his mother's voice lecture him about his posture. *I'm slumping over because I'm not into it,* he thought. *I didn't want to work in a large company like Dad did.* Immediately he heard his father talking about the benefits, retirement, and all the reasons to join a large organization. *Why doesn't it seem right for me?*

As he entered the elevator and jostled for a position as others crowded in, David thought about his job. Strangely, he was finding his work slightly more interesting with each day. It still didn't excite him, didn't have him jumping up out of bed in the morning, but things were now somewhat tolerable. His boss even had complimentary things to say one afternoon, or at least that's the way David interpreted it. David forced out of his mind the one comment that he wasn't seen as "future leadership." David was deeply committed to his team, and he wanted to make sure that they achieved their goals regardless of what he was feeling. Still, the worry over possibly losing his job gnawed at him. He knew that the warning was still in his personnel file, which felt like a never-ending itch he couldn't scratch. Despite this near constant concern, he worked hard. Engrained in him from a young age was a work ethic that would make any parent proud.

His first meeting after lunch was at least one he looked forward to. It was about a project he enjoyed with a colleague whom he would describe as a friend. Deeply engaged in the conversation, with a whiteboard filled with colorful ideas, David felt energized. As the two colleagues talked, David glanced out the window and noticed a woman across the street from his office building. She was maybe seventy, dressed smartly, and it seemed like she was staring right at him. When he looked again, she was gone.

As he left the office, he couldn't help but glance at the spot where she had been standing earlier. Then, pushing her from his thoughts, he crossed the street, following his normal pattern home past the old theater. But then there she was. She was on the corner, motioning him over. David immediately wondered who she was and whether she was somehow connected with the Old Man, the mistakes, and if she had any answers to his many questions.

At first she stood motionless, then disappeared down some stairs. David ran over and noticed a door below street level. It was slightly ajar, and both light and music were spilling out into the early darkness. *I can't believe I'm doing this*, David said to himself before bounding down the stairs and pushing the door open.

"Close the door, please," a voice from across the hallway said, "and please have a seat."

He sat down on a comfortable couch. A fireplace was burning in the far corner, casting a warm glow into the room. He could feel the heat mixing with the outside air. A bookshelf lined the wall beside him, and he nonchalantly began to notice various titles. None of them looked familiar.

What am I doing here? This is crazy, David thought. Only a few weeks ago, he would never have been in this room. He wouldn't have walked down those stairs, wouldn't have sat here, wouldn't have even noticed the woman on the street. It seemed that his curiosity was increasing each day. The questions kept coming. His mind played his conversation with the Old Man over and over again.

She entered with a dexterity that belied her age. In her right hand, she balanced a tray with steaming cups of tea. Before he could offer to help, she had the tray on a table and was handing him a cup, asking if he wanted milk or sugar, before settling on a chair opposite his.

"Let me introduce myself," she said and then launched into a quick explanation. She was speaking so normally, so casually, so calmly that it was as if everything was happening exactly as she expected, as if conversations with strangers walking off the street were everyday occurrences. "Right now, we are sitting in what used to be the private quarters of the original owner of the building. Above us, you may know, is one of the oldest theaters in the city."

"No, I didn't know. I'm not quite sure what I'm doing here and what this is about. Are you an actress?"

She laughed easily and ignored part of his inquiry. "I was at one point, yes, but for many years I have written—all sorts of plays, some of which you may know. Several left this theater and were turned into movies."

Now it came to him. She was the Playwright. The city treasured her creativity, and he had seen several of her plays and at least one of those movies. Thoughts scrambled for attention: *She's one of the most celebrated talents anywhere, and here I am engaging in a conversation with her as if this happened every day. She has to be connected to all of this. Why now? Why here?*

The Playwright sipped her tea, her hands wrapped around the small cup as if it brought life itself. For a few moments, they both drank tea and said nothing. David would ordinarily be very uncomfortable in the silence, but something about her was calming. It felt good to be with her, her presence somehow easing his spirit and eliminating his doubts.

A thousand questions were running through his mind, jumbled up together. He didn't know where to begin. Just when he was about to break the silence with a question, the Playwright said in an authoritative tone, "It's time. Let's begin."

And without any fanfare or introduction, without any reference to the Old Man or the woman in the park, she said they were going to talk about the first mistake. "It's the mistake that most people not only make, but they cannot seem to move past. Its grip strengthens with each passing year."

She then took a deep breath, smoothed her blazer, and looked intently at David. "I made this mistake for far too long. Oh, how I wish I had known earlier what I know now. And someone tried to tell me, but I wouldn't hear. Maybe I couldn't hear; I don't know."

She seemed lost in thought, in the past, recalling some distant memory. "But what an amazing opportunity for you to learn this so young!" Her voice increased and her passion for the subject was evident.

David realized he hadn't taken a breath. His anticipation for the first mistake was more intense than he'd thought.

She continued, "The first mistake is one that is so easy to make. It happens so quickly and yet so subtly that most don't notice." She frowned as she said that and then pulled out a small book.

David's eyes lit up. It was the same small book that the Old Man had had with him in the café. He was almost sure of it. At least it looked that way. He tried to peer into it from his chair but couldn't make out anything.

"You were right," she said, "I was an actress. I was, they say, quite good back in the day.

"It wasn't until I turned thirty that I realized what had happened in my life. My roles were written by someone else, and I was playing a part. I guess that's obvious since I was acting, isn't it?"

She didn't expect an answer but then said, "It may be obvious for an actress, but it isn't as obvious for most people. All of us are playing a role. We are acting out a part that was cast for us by someone else, for something unknown. We don't even notice it."

She smiled as she realized she was getting louder. "Come upstairs."

Without waiting for a response, she was on her feet and moving. David set his cup of tea down and tried to keep up with her. At the bottom of the staircase, he noticed framed pictures, all of which had the Playwright's name beneath. She clearly was a more accomplished actress than she had indicated.

At the top of the stairs, she turned left, and David found himself backstage. He tried to silence his internal voice, which was questioning this entire meeting. He deliberately shifted his thinking, ignoring the internal questions, and watched the action onstage. Booming voices echoed through the theater. Play practice was in full swing. The two of them were standing at a perfect observation point. After several minutes watching, the Playwright turned and spoke in a voice just above a whisper.

"It was a very difficult decision in my life. I had to decide whether to leave acting. I just couldn't do both, so I finally did it. I took up writing and left acting behind when I learned the first mistake. Now, please don't misunderstand. There is absolutely nothing wrong with acting. It's a wonderful profession. But listen carefully to what I am saying." She stopped, searching for the right words. "When you act, you are fitting into the story. When you write, you are creating your own story."

She looked deep into David's eyes. Her own eyes were misty.

"The first mistake is working on someone else's dream."

There was a long silence. Even the rehearsal, though completely unaware of this conversation, fell silent at that moment. "Most of us play a part in someone else's play. We dutifully learn our lines, our expressions. A life choreographed by someone else is not your finest performance.

"Think about going to work each day. You are working for someone else. You're doing what they want. If you don't, you're fired. Of course, you don't need to start your own business if that's not your calling. But the key is that you decided on your own—that it was a deliberate decision—and not that you just fell into a job, toiling away and playing a supporting role in someone else's play."

The Playwright was delivering these lines with a passion combined with empathy, and it was not lost on David that she was a powerful orator. He could almost feel her words and their impact inside his being. As she talked about getting fired, he felt something inside stir. Her comments lit a match to an internal fear that was never far from the surface.

"Your purpose is unique. No one else on the planet is like you. Your purpose is what energizes you. Design your life to fulfill your purpose. The clearer your purpose, the faster it will be attained. A clear purpose attracts people, ideas, and resources to its cause."

She paused, looking at David, who was leaning in and listening intently. She was clearly pleased at having his rapt attention.

"Don't allow someone else to make you an unwitting participant in their plan. Be a part of your own plan. Write the story of your future. Be the hero of your story, not a minor character in someone else's. It's so important you take the time to determine who you want to become, not just what you want to do."

David's eyes darted to her hands and the book. She was

cradling it, almost caressing its cover. Her eyes wandered back to the stage when the action began again. His gaze followed hers. He was enjoying the unusual backstage pass and a vantage point rarely seen by someone outside the business.

By the time he glanced back to her, she was gone. He hadn't noticed her leave. He thought maybe she'd excused herself and would return, but the practice ended and she still had not come back. He retraced his steps, back down the stairs, down the hall, and into the room where they'd started. The fire was nearly out, and there was no sign of the Playwright. He put on his jacket, went up the stairs, back to the busy street, and began walking to the park to go home.

Curiouser and curiouser, he thought. Though the Playwright had vanished, her words rang inside him. Someone else's dream? David thought of a friend who was now working in the family business because that's what was expected. Then he remembered another who wanted desperately to change her major, but couldn't find the will to fight her mother's wishes. *I wonder when most of us start following someone else's dream?* David caught a glimpse of himself in a shop window and smiled when he saw the seriousness of his expression. *Well, the Old Man will be pleased that I'm taking this seriously, that's for sure,* he thought.

When he arrived home, he took off his jacket and noticed a piece of paper sticking out of his pocket.

MISTAKE #1:
Working on Someone Else's Dream

Don't act out a part cast by someone else. You are the casting agent of your life's purpose.

A life choreographed by someone else is not our finest performance.

Your purpose is unique.

Design your life to fulfill your purpose.

A clear purpose attracts people, ideas, and resources to its cause.

Don't be an unwitting participant in someone else's plan.

Be the hero of your story, not a minor character in someone else's.

Determine who you want to be, not what you want to do.

MISTAKE TWO

For some reason, David thought he would have a sleepless night—with too many thoughts swirling in his head jockeying for position and aiming to have his full attention. He would think about the Old Man, the Playwright, then about a work project, then a friend, and then back to something else. But no sooner did he get under the covers than he fell fast asleep.

The next thing he knew, light was streaming in around the blinds in his room, prodding him awake. He felt incredibly rested, calm. The air was still, and he reveled in the unusual silence. What was it that the Old Man had said about silence? It speaks wisdom. He smiled as he thought about it, then remembered the first mistake.

Am I working on someone else's dream? What is my own dream? What is my purpose?

He wondered about his job. Why was he so worried about losing something he didn't even enjoy? And how could he recapture the excitement he'd had only a few years before?

Questions kept popping into his mind, one by one, as if

appearing on a screen in his brain. He thought about each one as he stretched, got up, brushed his teeth, and dressed for his morning jog. He was out the door before his mind could stop his body.

The fall air was noticeably cooler today. Thinking a slow run would clear everything out of his mind, he was surprised when he couldn't stop thinking about the bills, stacked silently in his kitchen. He thought about his boss, about his coworkers, about his life. For some unknown reason, he thought about his father's midlife crisis, how the sports car appeared one day in their driveway, signaling its onset, and how it disappeared sometime later with little fanfare. They had talked about it once; his father had made light of it, but the same questions his father was asking then were already at work in David now, born years too early.

Returning home, he felt the tiredness mixed with the endorphins from his run. The cold didn't bother him now and didn't slow his mind from its relentless questioning of everything.

He wanted to find the Old Man. He wanted to force it all out of him. He imagined himself grabbing the book, thumbing through its pages, reading and learning all of its wisdom.

David showered, dressed, and looked in the full-length mirror hung on the back of his closet door. He then undressed and started over. He wasn't usually this particular, but he wanted to look more presentable for his appointment today. He needed to ask for a loan. At the thought of the bank, he could feel a burning in his gut, a fiery reminder that he had stumbled financially. When he was finally satisfied with his appearance, he exited the bedroom.

The sun warmed the small living room with a saucy gold tone. He grabbed his folder and his leather bag, the one he had received as a new employee welcome gift, and then left for the bank.

He stepped onto the sidewalk and dodged strangers, all on

their way to somewhere, all with the hurried pace of purpose and determination. He saw a young mother balancing a child on her hip while maneuvering a stroller with the other hand. An older gentleman, and that's exactly what he looked like, complete with a polished cane and hat, passed him. David walked up the block, nearing the café where he'd first met the Old Man. He told himself not to look in the window this time. Of all days, this was not the day to find the Old Man. He didn't know if he could control himself, so great was his desire to know the truth of it all. When he reached the café, he looked anyway, but the sun's reflection blocked any view of the inside. Just as well.

David rounded the next corner and saw the bank in front of him. He paused. There was no real reason to be nervous. It was his bank. Sure, he had bills piling up, but he wasn't in dire straits yet. Maybe he should just go to work and forget it.

He must have been gawking at the door a little too long. An impeccably dressed middle-aged woman swung open the door. In a professional, courteous voice, she invited him inside. All of a sudden, he felt ridiculous, wondering how long he had stared at the building while second-guessing his clothes and fidgeting with his bag.

"It's warmer in here," she said. "And if you want to admire the art, feel free to take a closer look."

David's brow furrowed in momentary confusion as he entered the bank's cavernous lobby. She was already moving, looking up and gesturing. It took him a moment to realize that she thought he had been admiring the massive painting from outside the bank's doors.

"Isn't it something? I never get tired of looking at it."

David glanced up and really saw what was in front of him. He was far from an art expert, but he had taken art history in school and, though he was better at talking sports, he was able to fake it well enough to fumble through a conversation.

"It is. I couldn't help but admire it from outside; the light pulled out colors I hadn't noticed before." As he said this, David silently wondered whether the light even hit the painting at all this time of morning.

Fortunately, the woman didn't argue or respond to his comment. Instead, she turned to him and said, "She's the best artist in town, and she custom-made this for us. This is what it looked like, on this land, when the town was first founded. Do you bank with us?"

"Yes, I do," said David, introducing himself and, recovering from what he thought of as a slow start, added, "You know, while I'm here, maybe I could talk about some of my financial needs."

She smiled brightly. "Needs and seeds, that's what we do here."

David registered her remark by raising his left eyebrow in a subtle but obvious show of confusion.

She giggled to herself and then added, "Sorry. That's what my grandfather used to say. You see some people come here with needs. They need a loan or some help. Others with seeds. They have a deposit or want to talk about investments. Seeds and needs. You saying 'needs' just triggered a distant memory. Let's go to my office."

David followed her. She was not at all what he pictured when he thought about coming to the bank, though he guessed he didn't really know what he had expected.

They crossed the bank's lobby and entered a large office. She motioned for him to sit down and offered him something to drink. He declined but picked up the conversation about her grandfather.

Tossing a comment into the air, he hoped to build rapport with her before asking for a loan. "He sounds like an interesting man, your grandfather..."

"Oh, he was!" she replied quickly, her face lighting up. "He was something! Full of lessons, too. Here, let me show you something he loved to share with our clients."

She walked over to a wall of shelves. Each shelf was full of knickknacks, pictures, and books. "Where did I...? Ah, yes, here it is." She was on the tips of her toes, reaching above her head, and then she pulled down an old container.

"This was my grandfather's. Well, handed down to him. It's an old butter churner pot, but he filled it with coins. I wish the coins inside were from the same time frame. An antique dealer told me the old pot is likely from the beginning of the country. I guess I should treat it better, but it's always been here."

David shifted in his seat, wondering where this was going and rehearsing his speech about consolidating his credit card debt.

She pulled out several pennies and nickels and spread them on the table between them. "You'll love this," and then, with no warning, she tossed two coins into the air at David. "If you catch them they're yours!"

David instinctively and expertly grabbed the coins from the air.

"Know what's amazing about them? Look at that penny. It costs far more to make a penny than a penny is worth. Isn't that crazy?"

"Really?" David said. "Then why do they make them?"

She waved off the question and went right for the lesson. "The label on the penny is supposed to declare the value, but the real value is not the label."

She looked at David expectantly. But David only stared back.

"OK. The penny is worth more than a penny—the nickel, too.

Last I checked, it costs almost twice as much to make the nickel than it is worth. But that label is on there, so we accept it, and that's what it is."

She was now on a roll. "It's like that in life. Others slap a value on you. Not management material! Not an athlete! Not a good public speaker. Not a writer. Not good with people. Not this, not that! And you know what? Your mind is a sponge. It doesn't know any better, so it accepts the wrong label."

David listened to her and nodded, beginning to understand.

"Amazing to hear a banker say that a penny is worth more than a penny, isn't it? Trust me, if you bring us a roll of pennies, we're not giving you more than face value!" she said, laughing. She suddenly stopped herself. "Oh, my goodness!" she said. "I haven't even introduced myself. I'm sorry. You're a client, but your name..."

"Is David," he said, smiling and feeling more comfortable than he dreamed possible. After telling her his account number, his job, and his background, he turned back to her.

"I suppose you know by now who I am." She handed him another coin and he felt its warmth. "And you may even know..." She paused, got up from the table, crossed over to the same bookshelf, and removed a well-worn, familiar book, "that meeting me is part of the plan."

David's eyes widened as he realized what was happening. He expected to hear about the mistakes, but this was beyond bizarre. "How could this happen? How could you have known I was coming?"

"I wish I knew how that all works," said the Banker. "Once the process begins, it's like the entire universe is reordered for your benefit. I think"—she rubbed her right temple in a circular motion before adding—"you can study that one later. Right now," the Banker said with a wink, "I want you to understand this mistake."

David could only nod. Then he shook his head for a second to pull himself back into the moment.

"Mistake number two is allowing someone else to define your value."

David looked at her, still completely in shock that this was happening. She continued, undaunted and unfazed by his disbelief.

"Back to the coins. The label on the coin doesn't reflect the value of the coin. And yet we believe the label is accurate. In life, we make a big mistake when we believe the labels others slap on us. So much of our potential is wasted because we believe what others say. And then it gets worse, much worse. We accept our *own* labels. We believe we can't run that marathon, can't lose weight, can't start our own business, can't get promoted, can't make a difference, can't hit our goals, can't become wealthy, can't, can't, can't! We believe that we are destined for a certain kind of life."

The Banker slowly turned very serious and looked right at David. "Nice for you to learn this when you're young. I didn't learn until I was much older, but whenever we learn the mistakes, we can change everything. I regret I lived much of my life by others' expectations and labels. When I was growing up, most people believed girls were not good with numbers. Even though math was my favorite and best subject, I believed them. I didn't take advanced classes in high school because I was told I wouldn't be able to keep up. I avoided the classes I wanted to take in college because I was convinced I would fail. It took a long time for me to realize they were wrong, and by then it was much harder to pursue the career in finance I wanted. But I managed and am much happier in what I do now. I just wish I had had more courage to be me when I was younger. I didn't. You need to realize this when you still have time. Regret is the result of any action pulling against our heart's purpose."

She let her words sit there for a bit. Just like the Playwright, she wasn't rushing, wasn't in a hurry. Instead, she was watching him closely, somehow discerning whether he was understanding. David sat there just taking it all in.

After a few minutes, she continued. "Others are so quick to define us. They set expectations. They don't realize when we've changed. They don't see our potential. Our parents, our siblings, our friends have us locked in time, seeing us one way and not seeing us for who we are or what we've become. Heck, even Jesus performed miracles and then went home, and the people he knew were like, 'Dude, isn't this Joseph and Mary's son? What's up with this?'"

She started laughing again loudly, genuinely happy in her storytelling.

"Maybe they didn't say it quite like that, but you get the point. A life well lived is a life true to who you are. Not who others say you are. It's about you."

David thought about the warning at work, how its negative label was sticking to his thoughts.

"Promise me not to let this happen to you," the Banker implored, as if through the sheer force of her willpower she could change David's innermost thoughts.

"Be true to yourself. Let nothing come between you and your purpose. Don't accept the limitations others put on you. Know your value."

A man peered into the Banker's office and then knocked twice on the side of the door. "Do you have the report? They're asking for it," he asked.

"Oh, excuse me, I will be right back." She picked up some papers from her desk, leaving David deep in thought.

David held the coins that the Banker had given him, studying them in a way that he hadn't ever done before. He thought about the value of these coins versus the labels and the powerful lesson he learned. It was one he hoped he would never forget. He also thought about needs and seeds. He realized that he wanted to be able to come to the bank with his seeds, not his needs. He laughed to himself; it sounded ridiculous.

She returned a few minutes later and apologized for leaving him.

"Now," she said. "You had some banking business you wanted to attend to..."

"I do," David said. "My long-term goal with this bank is to be an investor, but right now, I want to get some advice on my credit cards..."

The two began to talk about ways to reduce his debt and turn his financial situation around. She was generous with her counsel and offered several ideas to help. She wrote down the titles of two books to get at the local library on budgeting. She gave him some paperwork to review for his credit cards and bills.

Escorting him out through the lobby, she smiled as she looked at him. "I'm so excited for you, David. It may seem dark now, but just you wait. Enormous power is possible when you give permission to be true to yourself."

Late that evening, as he sat on his comfortable sofa at home, he pulled out the paperwork she had given him and rifled through it. The last page was the one he was looking for. He read it several times.

MISTAKE #2:
Allowing Someone Else to Define Your Value

A life well lived is a life true to yourself.

Let nothing come between you and your purpose.

Don't accept the limitations others put on you.

Regret is the result of any action pulling against our heart's purpose.

Know your inherent value.

Enormous power is possible when you give permission to be true to yourself.

⌘⌘⌘

So much had happened since Aria had started her journey the night before, and she tried to tamp down the emotions she was feeling: worry for her uncle, confusion over Alexander's appearance at her home at such an hour, and stress from the weight of her purpose now firmly on her shoulders. Knocking on the door, she said another quick prayer for her uncle.

Her uncle's beloved friend greeted her and ended her short-lived hope that perhaps all was well.

"I thought you were still asleep. I didn't realize you were out," Robert said, not questioning directly, but the look in his eyes did little to hide his curiosity about her whereabouts.

"Yes, I went for an early morning walk in the woods. To clear my head." Aria strived to always tell the truth, but she didn't dare share more information against her uncle's wishes. *And I have been on a walk in the woods,* she thought to herself.

Robert glanced at the box she had tucked under her arm but seemed to accept her story, or he lacked the will to pursue it further. "Well, he's been asking for you. He actually said he will not die until he sees you again," he said, an air of sad resignation in his voice. She thanked him, only partially present in the moment, the other part of her still at the fire. The news would arrive at some point, but for now, she said nothing. She took her leave and moved toward the bedroom.

She heard her uncle's labored breathing even before she entered his room. At least he had survived the night.

Aria pushed the door open, the hinges' squealing announcing her presence.

Her uncle's piercing, questioning eyes met hers. She looked down, afraid of losing him.

"You have it?" he asked with a surprisingly strong voice, though the usual baritone was replaced with a raspy tone.

She nodded. "How are you...?"

He silenced her with a wave of his hand. "Let's not waste the precious time and words I have left on my condition. I'm glad it's here," he said, gazing at the box.

She looked at him again, and instead of feeling the weight of responsibility, she only felt a deep love for the man who had taught her everything worth knowing. She smiled at him, willing herself to be strong.

"The manuscript must be protected. It represents tremendous power, and I still need to..."

Midway through the sentence, he coughed loudly, a spell that lingered for a few minutes. The strength she had seen in him now seemed to wane as he gasped for a breath and his eyes closed.

She walked closer to the bed, took his hand, and then stroked his face, tracing the weathered lines of a life now ebbing. He must have been up all night, worrying. Only a minute later his eyelids closed, heavy, and seconds later he was asleep. Aria knew not how long he would live. She wanted to ask him what to do, where to go, and how and whether to warn the Nine.

She slumped into a chair next to the bed, pulling a small blanket up to her chest and maintaining a vigil. Her uncle's presence and his rhythmic snoring somehow soothed her nerves. Exhausted, Aria dozed off herself.

In her dreams, her mind replayed her first meeting with Alexander. Alexander was thrust into her life with such power, an unexpected surge of energy. He was tall, imposing, his smile bright and yet slightly off center. He had only recently moved into town, a former soldier, who left the army with distinction and unusual humility since he would talk so little about his own wounds in service. Now he was working as an apprentice and learning a new trade. His left arm and shoulder clearly gave him trouble, but his injury did not define him. Their first glance turned into a gaze and seemed to her like destiny, something she had longed for.

Her uncle welcomed the courtship and, as she pictured these last few weeks, she mostly remembered the laughing. He was a master storyteller and regaled her with tales from distant lands. Now all of it was suspect. Was everything that had happened these last few weeks a ploy to get close to her and then steal her uncle's book? What else could he have been doing in the middle of the night? She tossed and turned, her unconscious mind searching for answers just out of reach.

In her dream, Alexander faded away, and then the other man came into the picture. She could see the marks on his skin, the oil in his hair, and she smelled the foulness of his breath as if he were right in front of her. It was like she was seeing him from an angle above. She shivered as she watched him, his sneer not hiding the evil within.

Who was this man?

She awoke in a daze, not recognizing the room, her vision slowly coming into focus.

She looked over to her uncle's bed and then leapt up. The bed was empty! And the manuscript box was missing!

The recognition of what happened stung her; though expected, it still caught her off guard. She put her hand on his pillow, which was still warm.

The door creaked open and she spun around.

Her mouth dropped open and yet no sound came out.

Uncle Raymond's eyes twinkled at her as he reached out and brushed a stray strand of her auburn hair from her face. As he did this, she reached for his hand and grasped it, not quite certain whether she was seeing an apparition or if a miracle had truly happened.

"I thought you were gone," she said, managing a smile, feeling for appropriate words.

Her uncle's mouth curved into that classic smile of his, the one she had feared she would never see again. For a moment, she thought perhaps she was still in her own bed, dreaming, imagining his visage.

His words soothed her. "Aria, the sickness tried to take me, but you know your old uncle. I'm not going anywhere until I'm ready and my work is done." His words and subsequent laugh were stronger than they had been in days, though she could hear the hoarseness still lingering. "I know I have limited time, but my hour has not yet come. There's still much to be done! And I can think of no one better than my beautiful, brave niece to accomplish the task ahead."

Aria blushed. Pushing a stray hair from her eyes, she turned to her uncle. "Uncle, I try to be brave at all times. I try to not doubt. I just want it to end soon. And I don't want to fail you."

In her uncle's eyes, Aria saw understanding. His head bobbed slightly up and down. "It's our duty to protect the secrets for now. The manuscript can change the balance of power."

"Uncle, there were many men arriving at the house. I'm not sure how you knew when they would be coming, but I made it just in time." She swallowed, not wanting to give voice to her fear of betrayal. "I think Alexander is involved somehow. I don't want to think it, but he was there with the other men this morning."

Uncle Raymond's eyes widened as he weighed this news. "One step at a time, my dear Aria." This new information was clearly unwelcome, and yet he didn't dwell on it. "We have much to do, much to do."

As her uncle said this, his gaze shifted over her left shoulder, through the paned glass onto the house gate. "I have sent a message to the Nine, but I must work on the transition. We need to retrieve the Three Laws of the Keeper."

"Three Laws of the Keeper? What?"

"Aria, the Keeper has a serious position as the leader and protector of the Nine. There are laws that are universal truths, but carry more power as a leader."

"Uncle Raymond, I love you. I do. I want to do what you ask, but I don't understand any of this. Everything is happening too fast. And you need to be resting—you still aren't well."

"Time is a swift current pulling us along with unmatched power. Much as we wish, we cannot stop or slow it. But let's not talk about this now. They'll be coming to tell us of the fire. Let them think I'm convalescing in bed. Let's go. Believe me, my friends can well handle them." He gestured out to the window overlooking the field in front of the house, and she saw the group of men immediately. Her heart jumped.

"That's one of them!" she said in a whispered but urgent tone. An involuntary shudder ran through her body. "He is the man who was speaking to Alexander."

Uncle Raymond followed her eyes and saw him. "That's Ulrick," he said flatly. "I'm not surprised. I sure hope Alexander isn't mixed up with the likes of him. He's been trying to get the book and learn its secrets for years now."

"Wait! Oh, no. There he is. Alexander is with him," Aria said in a whisper with more than a hint of sadness in her voice.

At that moment, a loud knocking started at the front door, urgent, demanding. Uncle Raymond made a sign with his hand, signaling quiet, and pointed to the far hall. She understood. Even as a little girl, they had rehearsed exits, escape routes, signals. He routinely scouted everything when he arrived in a new building. She used to think that it was all for her entertainment, games invented to amuse her.

Now she knew differently. She had seen it for herself. Preparation meant everything. She shouldn't be surprised that he had mapped out this home long before. She found herself doing the very same thing, the result of a lifetime with her beloved uncle Raymond.

With a shake of her head, she followed her uncle. He took a slight deviation from the normal route to the back door, slipping to the right. He pulled one of the framed pieces of art off the wall and tucked it under his arm. It was smaller than the other pieces, and oddly out of place now that she was paying attention.

She prayed to the Almighty as they slipped out the back entrance, thanking God for her uncle.

⌘⌘⌘

MISTAKE THREE

Months passed. David was busier than ever at work. He thought often about the Old Man, the Playwright, and the Banker. He regularly reviewed the loose pages he'd been handed. He began making notes in a journal, writing his own thoughts about his life and his purpose:

I realize now that joining this company wasn't my dream. My father wanted me to choose a big company. My college professor pushed this opportunity. Where I wanted either a small company or even to start my own venture.

But it wasn't just him. I always felt I didn't have the right skills. I'm not good with money, and you need money to start a business. But after talking with the Banker, maybe it's not that I'm bad with money; maybe I just need to learn how to manage my finances. It still feels like a big risk, but is it worth it?

Not good: micromanaged, office politics, boring days full of meetings.

Good: creative brainstorms, small groups, fast pace.

I'm determined to make a difference and have an impact.

A few days later, David was attending a company-wide meeting in a hotel ballroom. He walked up to the registration table and picked up a marker to write his name on a name tag. As soon as he did, he thought again about the second mistake. As he listened to the speaker, David's mind wandered, and he reviewed all of the labels unfairly put on him. Exiting the meeting, he stopped by the table and asked if he could have a few of the extra blank name tags. "Sure, here's a whole pack."

Back in his office, David decided to write up his own labels. He realized it would seem over-the-top to some, but it seemed right to him. He started to write some of the negative labels he had heard about himself through the years. Whatever negative word popped into his mind, he wrote it down. Several were labels from his current boss. "Not a leader" echoed in his mind. *That's practically just calling me a total loser.* After a while, David thought about the positive labels he had heard through the years. And he thought about the labels he aspired to hear. He started to write down more labels, one on each name tag: "Successful." "Leader." "Strong." "Encouraging." "Mr. Positive!" "Upbeat." "Kind." "Giving." "High-energy." "Great friend." "Grateful." "Best boss ever."

David paused and then wrote "Millionaire" on the next tag. He thought about it, stifled a laugh, and then added "Multi-" to the front of the card. *Why not go for it?*

Gathering up the negative labels, David got up from his desk and walked over to the office shredder. He ceremoniously began shredding each of them. This type of thing was not at all like him, so he was surprised at himself when he realized he was smiling from ear to ear as he walked back to his desk.

"I am literally choosing my own labels now," David said to himself. "I wonder what the Old Man would say!"

He thought of the mistakes often, but no one else had approached him. Though he ate at the café, walked in the park, even visited the hospital, he saw no sign of anything unusual. He pondered the mystery of it all and whether he would ever learn the other mistakes.

David was at the gym late one Monday afternoon. He had started a routine of going at least three times a week. A few of his colleagues from work would go, too, and he had met many people while working out. Truth be told, he often found himself socializing as much as exercising.

That's when he met the Trainer. Actually, he first met the Trainer's girlfriend at the little shop when he was buying a protein shake. He couldn't help but notice how she moved with power, with an energy that eluded him. David was going through the motions, tired, trying to get through his routine at each visit. She, on the other hand, seemed to enjoy the gym as much as breathing. They exchanged a few words and then her boyfriend, the Trainer, walked in.

He was one of those guys who seemed to be in perfect shape. Not overly muscular, but it was obvious that he was not flesh and bone. No, he was clearly chiseled from a block of marble. He wasn't overtly showing it off, either, not wearing a shirt two sizes too small or anything obnoxious.

David looked at the couple and sensed the physical energy from both of them. The Trainer asked about David's workout and received a mumbled reply.

The Trainer asked again, and David demurred, "I don't have time to work out all day like you must. I'm busy at work. My job is stressful. I never have enough time."

It sounded lame leaving his mouth, but David was trying to

move on now, looking for a polite way to exit the conversation and head home. The Trainer's girlfriend excused herself, saying she had to return to work, and the Trainer pushed a chair out opposite from him with his foot. "Have a minute? Let's talk," he said, and it seemed more of an order than a question.

David slumped into the chair, not really ready for a lecture, preparing himself for what he knew would be a personal training sales pitch. When he first joined the athletic club, one of the salespeople would not leave him alone. The last thing he wanted was to go through that again.

The Trainer asked, "Are you happy with your body? Are you healthy? Are you achieving your goals?" He smiled and then went silent.

With a deep exhale of a breath, David answered, only to get more probing questions from his new friend. The Trainer wasn't judging, wasn't selling. He was only listening.

"Sure, if I was a bodybuilder and trainer, I would spend all day here and look like you. But I'm not and I can't," David said and then looked up. "My job is all consuming. I wish I had more time. It takes all my energy just to get in here at all."

"I'm not a professional trainer here," he said, "and I'm not a pro bodybuilder, either."

David, clearly surprised, received this as a jolt to his system. "You're not? What do you do?"

"It doesn't matter, really. I do have a training business—but it's not physical training. I do organizational consulting and corporate training."

David rubbed his temples with both hands, embarrassed that he had pegged the guy incorrectly. His body heat soared, and his face flushed crimson red. "Sorry, I think I made a few bad assumptions. It's just, well, the way you look made me think…" He stopped himself midsentence and changed course. "Okay. So, what's your story? And how can you look like that if you're *not* a weight lifter and trainer?"

His request opened up a completely different conversation. David learned more about the Trainer. He had grown up the youngest of three brothers and was often picked on. He struggled in school. When he was a senior in high school, he ended up fighting leukemia and for his life.

"I was anything but an athlete. I was in and out of the hospital. I had treatment after treatment. Some days, I look back, and it's all a blur, and other days I realize it was the most incredible thing, the best thing that ever happened to me."

"Why?" David blurted out, then softened it a bit by adding, "How can that be the best thing that ever happened?"

"When I was in for a treatment one time, I met someone. She finished her cancer treatments and made it her goal to compete in a triathlon." As he said this, exactly half of his face broke out into a grin.

"I couldn't believe it, but she actually won. Then she invited me to a special event. I didn't know what it was, but here she was speaking about her ordeal and about how it motivated her to grab life for all it's worth. Somehow, she turned her illness into a shot of motivation."

The Trainer finished his workout shake and then lobbed his napkin into the air. It landed neatly in the trash can at the opposite side of their table. "Impressive," David said, "and of course you would make it. I would miss every time."

"Why?"

"Because I'm not that coordinated. Heck, I go to brush my teeth and miss half the time," David said, laughing at his own humor.

"You sound like I did," the Trainer stated. "She tried back then to get me to run and to talk about my experience. She tried to get me to do a lot of things. But I always had a ready list of reasons why I couldn't do anything."

The Trainer looked at David with such laser-like focus that it unnerved him. He shifted his gaze to the two kids sitting with their father at the next table.

"Excuses. Behind every excuse is a door to greatness. When we learn to overcome the excuses that are preventing our progress, we begin an almost magical process of growth," the Trainer added before reaching quickly into his pocket. The Trainer looked down at something out of sight and then continued.

"That triathlon winner changed my life." The Trainer was smiling, recalling something unspoken. "She taught me not to accept excuses. People say, 'I'm too fat. I'm too thin. I don't have the right education. I'm afraid. I'm too this, too that.' Oh yes, my favorite: 'That's just not me.' Or, 'That's great for you, but I'm not wired that way.' "

"Let me guess. That woman is now your girlfriend?" David said, sure that he had connected the look in his eye.

"That's funny," the Trainer said. "She would love that!" The Trainer started laughing, then said, "But you're close. That woman is my girlfriend's grandmother!"

The creases in David's forehead conveyed his confusion, but the Trainer said, "See, that's just it. At her age, you would think she would be in a nursing home somewhere. And yet, there she was, running in her first triathlon and winning for her age group. She taught me not to listen to the voice inside that doubts and that questions, and instead tune in to the voice that encourages."

At that moment, the Trainer lifted a small leather book from under the table. David suddenly realized what was happening. He should have seen it coming, but it had been too long since he had last heard of the mistakes.

"Mistake number three is accepting excuses. If we put the energy and creativity into our goals that we put into creating excuses, we would achieve anything we set our minds to."

The Trainer didn't stop. "I could have blamed my illness, blamed my genes, and whined about my lost childhood or about my limits. No one would have stopped me. In fact, they would have nodded and agreed. People not going anywhere encourage excuses. But the only person who would have lost would have been me. I can't imagine where I'd be or what I would have become had I not learned this mistake at just the right time."

David took a deep breath and willed himself into serious listening mode. The mistakes were part of his life now, part of his thinking. He soaked everything in like a sponge and wanted to know more. The two talked for another hour, sharing more and becoming genuine friends.

What became very clear was that the Trainer wasn't really talking about physical fitness. "Excuses are everywhere. In the office, when someone doesn't make excuses, when they take full responsibility, it gets noticed. Know anyone like that?"

Immediately, David thought about one of the managers at the firm. She'd started only a few weeks before him but was promoted after only a short stint. "Yes, I think I do. One of our managers. She fits that description."

"What phrases does she say that make you think that of her?"

"She's said, 'I've got this, don't worry.'" David smiled, remembering another line. "Once, when something big blew up at work, I was panicked that I'd get the blame. For no reason, really, I wasn't even involved. But sure enough, she walks right in and says, 'Oh yes, that was all me. Sorry about that. Here's what we're going to do...'" David trailed off, thinking back.

"Exactly what I mean. A person who doesn't make excuses isn't afraid of accountability. In fact, they thrive on it. That's what you noticed."

"I wouldn't have thought of that," David responded. "Don't get me wrong. She's impressive, yes, but I could never figure out why she was given so much authority so quickly."

"Now you know," the Trainer said, adding, "A big part of not accepting excuses is changing your self-talk. Each of us has a microphone inside our head. It's the most important microphone in the world, but we leave it unguarded. We let anyone step up and just blast us with negativity. The most successful people, the ones who don't accept excuses? They guard that microphone like they're security at a bank vault."

As David was listening, he noticed his own self-talk. It wasn't full of confidence. In fact, it was far from it, filled with self-doubt and fear. Most of it was negative. He replayed a few lines in his memory and shook his head. "I hear you," David said, admitting, "I don't think I've guarded it so well, even against myself."

"That's why this one is so important and its impact so incredible. You see, excuses cannot withstand positive self-talk. If you want to take your life back, take your thoughts back."

With a fist bump and slap on the back, the Trainer disappeared, leaving David there surrounded by the noise of the gym's café. Somehow he had tuned it all out and was blissfully unaware of all of the activity around him. David began to listen to his inner voice.

Closing his eyes, even in the middle of the busyness of the gym, he imagined the microphone inside. When he heard an excuse, he imagined the speaker at a microphone. He invented a character who was doing the talking, gruff, grumpy, and weak. He imagined a strong version of himself, powerful, confident, grabbing the microphone forcefully and seizing control of the stage. He then spoke into the microphone with power and assurance. Words of encouragement and of accomplishment.

He smiled to himself and opened his eyes. David glanced about to see if anyone was watching, but no one was paying any attention to him.

Finally, he stood up to leave and looked down to realize that the Trainer had left a piece of paper for him.

MISTAKE #3:
Accepting Excuses

Avoid people who encourage excuses.

When we learn to overcome the excuses that are preventing our progress, we begin an almost magical process of growth.

Behind every excuse is a door to greatness.

People not going anywhere encourage excuses.

Tune out the voice that doubts and questions in favor of the one that encourages and convinces.

Shift the energy and creativity from creating excuses to achieving goals.

Guard your inner voice like you would your most precious treasure.

Excuses cannot withstand positive self-talk.

If you want to take your life back, take your thoughts back.

MISTAKE FOUR

David walked slowly back from the gym that night and not only because the snow was slickening the pavement. He was lost in thought, making mental lists of excuses. At first he was thinking about his fitness goals, but he realized that the third mistake went far beyond that. How many times, he thought, had he not tried for a promotion or not started something he should have because of an excuse? It wasn't hard for him to recall dozens of examples, and he found himself shaking his head as he walked. He thought about the ongoing struggles he was having at work and how worthless his job felt. Was he just making excuses? Was his purpose connected to his job at all?

That night David had planned a get-together with his friends. He glanced at the time and realized he would have about an hour at home before he needed to head back out. Walking into his apartment, he flicked the switch for the light. Nothing. He crossed the living room and tried another light. Nothing. He closed his eyes.

"Well, that's just great," David said aloud, constraining his language. He knew what it was. He had sent the electric bill payment the day it was due, but it likely hadn't been processed in time. He spent the next hour on the phone pleading with them. "Yes, of course, I should set up automatic payments. I just haven't gotten around to it." As he said it, David knew how lame it sounded. The truth was he was often playing these payment games, which would be impossible if his payments were automated.

Finally, the service representative agreed to temporarily restore his service. He hung up and felt pathetic, sitting in the darkened room. He stared at the far wall. "I will not live like this," he said. The only answer he heard was a horn on the street, reminding him he should leave and meet his friends.

They met at an old pub in town to sip beers and share some appetizers. He was trying to temporarily push away the fact that he had no electricity at his place. He wasn't about to share that with anyone. Mixed into his thoughts were the lessons from the Trainer. Frankly, they annoyed him at the moment. His mind was working overtime on justifiable excuses for his bill problem, and yet the Trainer's lessons didn't allow them any room. He shifted his attention to the conversation in front of him.

"My boss is such an idiot!" his friend Joe said, adding, "He's constantly telling me to do one thing; then he changes his mind and has me doing something else. So I end up not finishing anything. Make. Up. Your. Mind!" He poked the air as he punctuated each word for effect.

Joe's girlfriend was with him and piled on. "Oh, yeah? I can top that. My last boss was so busy sucking up at work that we thought that was his full-time job! No one could ever get anything done because he was never around, but it's not like we minded." Everyone laughed.

"Dude," Lonnie said, "if they don't give me a raise soon, I'm going to freak! This place doesn't pay enough. I'm telling you, I gotta get outta there."

David was listening but realized he was slightly removed, his mind working on something just out of reach. Every bit of whining, complaining, and justifying, he realized, was really mistake number three. Each complaint was a mask for an excuse. *That's it. Whining is a mask designed to hide an excuse. Starting now, I'm going to take responsibility for my actions.* As he was thinking these thoughts, David felt something shift inside him. So much so that his friends noticed.

"David. Earth to David. Come in, David," Joe joked, using his hands to enhance the volume of his voice as if he were an announcer. They all laughed. David felt himself with them, but he also realized that all of this self-reflection and the lessons of the mistakes took him elsewhere. He was on a journey, and the people sitting near him didn't even know he'd left.

After an hour of conversation, David's friends began to leave one at a time. David decided to move to the bar and catch the last of the game before heading home.

The Bartender approached him and took his order. They bantered back and forth. David watched the Bartender cut one unruly patron off from drinking and then stop a fight between two other customers. He admired how the man told stories and jokes to get others laughing. He was clearly a pro.

As the game continued to play, David and the Bartender struck up a conversation.

"I bet you see it all," David said. "I watched you tonight. You wear many hats: server, bartender, priest, comedian; you're a one-stop shop."

The Bartender laughed and took a slight bow. "Caught! You got me," he said in an Irish brogue that sounded remarkably authentic. "You *could* say that I see it all"—he was nodding his head—"and most people would learn a lot from what I see!"

David's eyes left the television screen. His team was so far ahead that it was game-over anyway. "What's the number one thing people could learn?"

The Bartender looked up. He was washing glasses behind the bar and was using some automatic brush machine to polish them one at a time before buffing them with a white cloth. He obviously took great pride in his work. The bar was pristine, everything gleaming, not a mark in sight, and the mirror so bright it looked brand-new.

"I'm no good at saying what's the best or number one anything. People ask me for the best drink, the best movie, the best dinner we offer. It's too hard to pick a number one."

"Well, tell me anything that pops into your head," David responded, hoping to prompt him.

"I have seen so much from behind this bar," the Bartender began, "the good, the bad, and the ugly!" He looked into the mirror as he said this and laughed at himself. "This could be a sitcom. Oh, wait, someone did that already!"

David laughed with him, and the Bartender continued.

"I've seen people with seriously messed-up lives. And then I've seen successful people. I guess I've seen successful people with seriously messed-up lives, too!" He laughed again, picturing someone in his mind.

"You know, I do think I have one for you," he said. "The wrong people. Yes . . . definitely, that's it."

He dried a glass, and then disappeared into the kitchen without another word. David watched him hoist a tray of food above his head and move to an unseen table somewhere behind him.

Not a minute later, he was back at the bar, counting money. David thought he would continue where he left off, but he didn't. Finally, David prompted him along back into the conversation.

"Tell me what you mean: 'The wrong people'?"

Lightly rubbing the stubble on the left side of his face, the Bartender looked at him, almost as if he didn't know what was being asked. He smiled, reached beneath the bar, and pulled out a familiar looking little book with a wink.

"I thought you'd never ask," he said. "Mistake number four is surrounding yourself with the wrong people."

He had a gleam in his eye and clearly enjoyed watching the surprised look on David's face. "I learned long ago that the people around us affect everything. Our friends determine our fate. Don't think it doesn't matter. Who you are around determines where you go."

David massaged his hands together. He didn't expect to hear the next mistake before he was finished processing the last mistake. And, as he listened to the Bartender, he just couldn't grasp what he was saying. To make it worse, David was thinking about the process again, about how these mysterious people appeared at seemingly random times.

The Bartender waved his hands in front of David. "Hello? Do you want to hear this?"

"Sorry," replied David, "I've been far away tonight. I know I should roll with it, but I'm still trying to understand this whole mistake thing. How do you know that I'm the one you should share this with, anyway? Why do I hear nothing for months and then suddenly two in one day?"

"Oh...we have one of *those*!" the Bartender replied with both hands in the air. "Seriously, you have to just take this all in right now. Don't question everything. If you do, you will miss what you need."

Shifting on his stool, David sighed and nodded. "OK, you win. Go ahead."

"Where was I? Oh, yes, who we are around. Our friends. It's incredible to study how influential those around us can be. I even read an article a few years back about friends gaining weight together. If a close friend gains a few pounds, chances are good you will, too. You know what's really strange about it?" the Bartender asked.

Shaking his head side to side, David found himself leaning in to listen closely.

"This happens even if they live hundreds of miles from each other. And if friends have that kind of influence over your weight, just think about what they are doing to your mind, to your opportunities, to your thinking. Think what would happen if instead of gaining weight together, you gained wealth together."

Once again, the Bartender left the conversation to attend to a few customers, leaving David to absorb the thought. A minute later, he was back and this time picked up the conversation immediately.

"And I've read a lot of about this phenomenon," the Bartender said. "Our friends influence everything: our choices, our thinking. It's amazing. Plus, would it surprise you to hear that people with close friends actually live longer?"

Not waiting for an answer, the Bartender said, "It's not too dramatic to say that who you are around determines your destiny. People may discount me spouting out here about what I've watched from behind this bar, but if they read the research, they would be stunned.

"I wasn't always a bartender. In fact, I worked in a big company, probably one like you do." As he said this, David felt his face redden involuntarily. The Bartender continued, "I had a wonderful experience and learned a lot, saved a lot. Then, my journey led me to experiment with many different jobs until I landed here. I've been here for years now, and I've never been happier. It's really *not* just about money, though most people don't know I own the place and two others just like it."

"Wow. I wouldn't have known that," David replied, thinking that he shouldn't be so quick to judge people based on appearance. "I thought a woman owned it."

"Most people don't know the history of this place," replied the Bartender. "It's actually been called Aria's for a few hundred years. It started as an inn. Story is that Aria wasn't the first owner, either, but under her ownership, it just boomed. You know, when I expanded the catering hall, I found some uniforms from the Revolutionary War. They're now displayed in the museum downtown. This place has an amazing history, lots of secrets. Many people on your same journey have sat in that very seat you're in."

David's hands caressed the wooden stool with a new appreciation. He traced the simple design and noted the sturdiness and handiwork of the craftsmanship. Not just the seat, but the entire tavern. He glanced into the restaurant, visible from a glass window behind him. He hadn't noticed the age of the place before.

The Bartender filled up two bowls with pretzels and assorted nuts and placed them in front of David. He topped off David's draft, creating the perfect foamy head with the flick of his wrist.

Then he switched the conversation back from the inn's history to the subject of friends and colleagues.

"Often we are more careful about the clothes we pick at a store than we are with the friends who determine our future." The Bartender shook his head. "Painful as it is, it's important to remember that, with kindness, we need to remove those who are dragging us down and find those who will pull us up. I guess it's like a formula.

"Years ago, people would smoke in here. Now most people want to avoid it at all costs. Yet they continue to breathe in toxic words from their friends. They hang around people who constantly complain and criticize. If they only knew. Replace the naysayers, the doubters, the energy drainers with the encouragers, the winners, the motivators. It doesn't have to be someone jumping up and down. It's much more subtle. And certainly not if someone is going through a temporary challenge. Then, lift that person up. Be the encourager and motivator they need. But if you find yourself consistently drained, it's time for a change."

The bartender smiled and handed David his check. "To me, it's the most important mistake of them all."

And, with that, he disappeared into the kitchen, happily humming a tune as he went.

David's mind was recalling the conversation with his friends. He remembered the complaining, criticizing, and making fun. He couldn't recall a single positive word. He thought about the people he was around at work, the ones encouraging him to keep his head down to get back into favor with the boss.

A thought crossed his mind, taking him back to his college days. He was happier and more confident then. Was that because his friends were, too?

Replaying the evening and all the negative comments, he realized he would need to make some changes. And none of them would be easy.

Here, I thought it was all about my job. But it may be about the people I'm hanging out with, David thought. *Maybe it's both.*

Everything around him seemed to get quiet, and the whole world seemed to slow. David realized not only had he been making excuses, but he was surrounded by people who were weighing him down. Beyond that, he realized he was going to have to leave his job. It really wasn't the boss or the hours. It wasn't the cube or the work. These were excuses; he knew that now from the earlier lesson. It was the simple fact that his purpose was bigger than the job allowed. As he came to this decision, he realized something else. He needed to find his purpose first, before leaving his job. He needed to pursue his dream from a position of strength and not from one of desperation. The lessons he had been reading over and over were so strongly in his subconscious mind that he felt emboldened. He felt... well, he felt... wise. And then he felt funny, at his age, for feeling wise.

David left cash on the bar before taking the paper that had clearly been left for him.

MISTAKE #4:
Surrounding Yourself with the Wrong People

Your friends determine your fate.

Who you are around determines where you go.

Don't spend more time picking out your clothes than picking out your friends.

Toxic people are often more dangerous and create more damage than we realize.

Replace naysayers, doubters, and energy drainers with encouragers, winners, and motivators.

Remove people from your life who consistently drain your energy.

Surround yourself with the people who will help you achieve your purpose.

THE FIRST LAW

⌘ ⌘ ⌘

Aria and Uncle Raymond left the house in the hope that their departure was undetected by anyone. They leaned on each other as they walked.

"What about your kind friends?" she asked as they finally disappeared behind a grove of trees, safely out of view. She knew where he was headed. The barn was to the left.

"Robert is difficult enough, but Mae is not one to be trifled with, trust me. She can handle more than the likes of them. And they'll think I'm asleep."

Arriving at the barn, he sat on a bench, which groaned as he lowered himself onto it. She thought they would be on their way immediately, but he had other ideas. He motioned for her to sit beside him.

Aria decided now was her chance to ask a question that had stayed with her. She had wondered about it but had never asked. "Uncle, all of the wisdom and lessons in that book...so much of it is known. And surely they cannot believe it has magical properties. So why do they want it really? Why must it be protected like this?"

Her uncle smiled, his eyes still closed. "Aria, that question has been asked for generations. It's true. A mistake may be known, but it's also true that it's mostly ignored. Many die with knowledge, but few have studied and applied that knowledge. It's the collection, in one place, with examples that make it a powerful force for those who apply it. Throughout the ages, many have sought its power to destroy others, to control, and for wrongful purposes. You can use the nine mistakes in a way that can manipulate. Some of it is still a mystery to me, Aria, but trust me, we're all better off keeping the nine mistakes safe.

"That is particularly true of this original manuscript, what I call the Keeper's copy. You see, this manuscript is different from the copies." Just when Aria thought she understood, she realized there was still more to know. He set the manuscript box between them, and then turned his attention to the picture he had taken off the wall.

"Years ago, I visited a printer and binder in town, and together we printed the nine books for the Teachers. The original manuscript, I kept as the Keeper. But there were three pages I left out of the printed version. We also modernized the language in the books, something done periodically to maintain the integrity of the message.

"You know what this is?" he said, motioning to the art piece.

"I've never paid any attention to that particular picture," she responded, searching her memory.

"I've hidden the three pages, Aria, in different places. I gave this piece as a gift to my friends. They never knew what was inside."

He turned the picture over, unfastened it, and then removed a single weathered page from the back. He paused for a moment, reverently, almost cradling it in his hands. "This is the first of the Laws of the Keeper." He looked at her. "There are two more hidden pages. Aria, I thought this would happen years from now... I'm sorry to give you this weight. You must now become the Keeper. I'm already on borrowed time." He gently handed the page to her.

Aria was stunned. Her world seemed at once to both open and close, like she was in a whirlwind of confusion.

The new Keeper? How was it possible to be the new Keeper? What about Uncle Raymond? What was he saying?

"Uncle, you're feeling well now. And I've only just learned from the Nine. Let's think about this. Maybe one of the Teachers..."

He held up his hand, in that way that Uncle Raymond did. Whenever he made that one motion, it seemed to stop the world. No one dared interrupt him when he did it from the judge's bench, and no one in his family ever did so, either. His hand would stop conversation faster than an orchestra conductor's movement would cease all musicians in a concert hall. She looked at him expectantly.

"It's time," said her uncle, "and I know that they won't suspect you in any way. Why, they would think me mad to give such power to a girl of your age. That's exactly why it will work. You're the last person they would expect."

"I'm nearly eighteen, Uncle," she said somewhat defensively while looking at scripted writing on the page.

"I know, you're a young woman now," her uncle responded. "I entrust you with the wisdom here, but I will always think of you—"

"As the little girl you first taught to ride," she interrupted, having heard him say it hundreds of times. He was always recalling how he taught her to ride a horse.

He looked at her with his kind eyes. "These books contain

the mistakes of the greats, of us all. Avoiding them early in life creates extraordinary power, often wealth, and always happiness. Keep them from falling into the wrong hands. Do you accept this task, the role of Keeper?"

Aria blinked and then nodded, mouthing the words he had asked for. "I accept." She held the manuscript box and the paper, knowing its weight, knowing all that it meant. It was a responsibility she would always carry.

"One day, we will defeat our enemies by releasing this wisdom into the world," he said. "That day will be something. Then we will succeed when we get word of the mistakes to everyone, especially the young, the ones starting over, and those who have the belief that they can still do something in this world of ours."

"When will that be?" she asked.

"It is not for me to know," he said, pausing. "Until then, we have strict rules for the succession. The Keeper is to make certain to protect the Nine from exposure and to ensure a successor for each. Use all of the wisdom you have in making that decision."

"What of the three laws?"

"The first is there in your hands, for you to read now. Remember, these pages are only for the Keeper. The simple wisdom is essential for anyone mastering all nine of the mistakes who aspires to choose those who will teach and who will receive the lessons. The Keeper has a high calling to leadership. Remember its message yourself as you make your own decisions. Read these laws often and heed the wisdom therein."

"I treasure all of it, dear Uncle, even if I don't understand it all fully," she said as she turned to him.

Uncle Raymond carefully placed the art piece inside the barn in a safe place. Then he asked her help in readying the horses.

Only a few minutes later, they were in a carriage headed away from the house, and she was able to read the page.

The Law of Desire

The Law of Desire is the first law. Desire is a spring overflowing to fill your life with goodness. All opportunity, all achievement, all power is activated first with a burning desire.

Desire the noble; think high thoughts; feast on the abundance of possibility. Guard against wasting your desire on the insignificant and small.

Only when your desire is great enough does it activate the winds of achievement to propel you to the impossible. Do not proceed without picturing your desires achieved fully. Your desire sets the course of your destiny.

Desire prevents others from limiting or labeling you unfairly. Desire pushes your thoughts to a new level, one higher than you think is possible. Let your desire burn within to fuel your success.

Aria contemplated the words and glanced at her uncle Raymond. He was driving the horse forward while still looking all around to make sure they were not followed. She didn't say anything for quite some time as they continued along.

Finally, she broke the silence. "Uncle, this law. Tell me more about it and the role of the Keeper."

He glanced over at her. "Aria, the three Laws of the Keeper are powerful leadership tools when used correctly. Desire, for instance, is an important starting point for all accomplishment. If you kindle a desire in a group dedicated to a cause, you create a move-ment. But if you use desire in the wrong manner, say for personal gain only, for selfish ambition, it is an entirely different matter." He stifled a yawn and continued. "I'm sorry for that. I guess I'm still worn down. In the wrong hands, it can be dangerous with heinous motives powering evil intention. Truth can easily be distorted, cre-ating manipulators who take advantage of those unaware."

Aria contemplated all of her uncle's words. She thought of Alexander and wondered about his motives. Had he been manip-ulated by Ulrick? Then, as they neared their destination, Aria asked her uncle what was ahead.

"I'm afraid that you will have to decide that now, my dear girl. My hope is that they don't suspect you and that the fire slows their pursuit. It will not likely deter their search forever. How to proceed will be a decision that only you will know."

They made it to his law offices in town, but the excitement had taken its toll on Uncle Raymond. As he pulled the carriage to the side, she helped him steady and tie the horses. His labored breathing reminded her that he had been deathly ill only hours ago. He needed to sit and rest, and she would need to force the issue. He reached into his pocket and pulled out a brass key. "Aria, this was meant for both of us. The Nine know this, and now you should. Before I took ill, I had made plans. In the chest in my office is the Second Law of the Keeper and enough money to start afresh. But you will need to decide what to do. I believe I am going on another journey soon, Aria. You can decide whether you can go on without me."

They were now inside his law offices, and Aria eased him onto a sofa in the parlor. Her mind was absorbing everything, weigh-ing options. Uncle Raymond rubbed his temples and yawned. "I've slept so much that I cannot possibly be tired again."

Aria looked at her uncle, and her mind registered his frail condition, his weakness. She had faced the worst and thought that he had miraculously been healed. Now she realized it was a temporary surge to accomplish his purpose and ready her for her mission.

"Uncle Raymond, I don't know where to start or what to say. I love you." She made no mention of the many questions swirling in her mind.

"I want you to know that I have every confidence in you," he said. "Now, go into my office and open the small chest, get what you need."

⌘⌘⌘

MISTAKE FIVE

He was being watched. David felt it. He glanced up and down the city street. Nothing seemed out of the ordinary. A couple was leaning close together, arm in arm. An older man was smoking across the street from them. With the next inhale, the cigarette lit up, and David noticed the orange glow brightening. Several other people were milling about, gazing in shop windows, going about their business.

He continued walking, at a leisurely pace, but still purposeful. David rarely strolled without an aim in sight. This time, he was heading to the bookstore in town. As he did, he still couldn't shake the feeling that someone was watching him. He wondered if it was the Playwright, since they had met at the theater not far from here. Turning left at the corner, he decided to walk by the theater, adding only a few blocks. It was closed, of course, this early on a Saturday. Tonight, hundreds would stand in line to enter and see the Playwright's newest production.

His feeling of being watched intensified as he turned the corner. A policeman, making his rounds, nearly collided with him. David quickly excused himself and dodged to the right.

A moment later, he was in front of the bookshop. The building had originally been constructed when this part of the city was first built, at the dawn of the country. He pulled open the thick wooden door, clearly an original piece complete with the original hardware. It groaned as it opened, and he felt the warm air rush out, pulling him inside.

He took a deep breath as he entered, his eyes adjusting to the light. He heard whispers from one of the aisles. The bookshop hadn't changed in years. It completely ignored the digital craze, the owner not only annoyed with technology, but stopping anyone who thought it was acceptable to use devices of any type in his store. It was a throwback to an earlier time. The town's library had long since embraced technology. It was a hub of conversation and excitement. But here, in this shop, the owner wanted nothing to do with the modern century. It was a wonder that the books weren't all classics. The striking differences between this and the other, modern bookstore in town was the subject of many news articles. Still, the owner had his loyal fans keeping the store afloat and successful long after many said he would go bankrupt.

Authors loved to visit the city, and they regularly had author signings in both locations. If you liked one bookstore, you weren't going to the other, so the two locations hosted completely different clientele.

David adored this place and all of its little quirks. It was always a shade too warm or too cold with no consistency, and it depended on which part of the store you were in. As he walked into one section, he was glad to have a scarf with him, and he wrapped it around his neck to block a cool breeze that seemed to be localized to the historical fiction section of the store.

He heard the door open and glanced back. He recognized the

face. She was beautiful, that was obvious, but he couldn't place her. How did he know her? She was clutching a bag and leaving the store before his mind recognized her. It was the young lady whom he first met in the park, the one who started this journey, responsible for the invitation to meet with the Old Man. He was momentarily stunned as the memory of that day flooded his senses.

He was quick to follow her out, hoping to catch her. Standing outside the door, he looked up and down the street, but she was nowhere to be seen. He stood for more than a few minutes, watching the pedestrians, hoping to spot her. After a while, he gave up and went back into the shop. He took a deep breath, realizing his heart was pounding from the excitement of seeing her again.

Calming himself, he went back to the aisles of books. He loved scanning the titles, as if by looking at the cover he could sense the story inside. David also loved to study book covers, the colors, the pictures, the design. He had purchased many books based solely on the cover alone. And, surprisingly, he wasn't often disappointed.

One book that grabbed his attention was about bad bosses and how to survive them. He smiled as he flipped it open, thinking that he should have read this some time ago. Fortunately, the warning from his boss was now history. By not making excuses or shifting blame, he was fast becoming one of the go-to talents in the organization. David learned he could even be a potential replacement for the manager, which was not at all what he'd expected. Yes, he was told it was a long shot, but just the fact he was told about it was a positive sign. He wondered if the newfound power he felt was from knowing he eventually wanted to leave the company despite any possible promotion. His purpose, his success, he now understood, was not related to corporate power or wealth.

David moved down the aisle, his eyes scanning the titles. At the back of the bookstore, he walked up a few stairs to another level. The building was ancient, and the stairs were tricky to navigate. Having been here before, he made his way through that room to an old solid cast-iron staircase. As he ascended the spiral stairs, he noticed the floral details in each step and he counted them as he ascended. Sixteen stairs later, he was in the room filled with what he considered "ancient" books.

Two steps into the room, he sneezed. The dust in here was layered so thick it was as if the owner spread some on each week to enhance the antiqueness of the room. He rubbed his left eye with his hand as his allergies started in full protest of the assault. As he did this, he noticed a middle-aged woman smiling at him from across the small room. He hadn't met her but was immediately sure he knew who she was. He had met her husband on his past visits, but that was usually on weeknights after work. It was "their" shop, but really, it was her baby, inherited from her mother.

"Bless you!" she said, adding, "I hope you're not allergic to books! If so, you're in the wrong place."

She said it as if she was completely unaware that the room was filled with dust and a strong old-book smell mingled with mold. Ironically, she was holding a rag and wiping a book. David immediately thought that the reason for his sneeze could be traced directly to her hand and the dust she had sent sailing into the air.

Deciding not to voice these thoughts, David simply met her gaze and smiled back. "Thank you. I have no idea what got into me," he said with a slight tone of sarcasm.

"Anything I can help you with?" she asked, ignoring or, more likely, oblivious to his veiled remark.

His standard "I'm just browsing" answer was there and ready, but he switched it off and instead found himself saying, "I'm not quite sure yet. I'm looking for something new."

She laughed and, like an actress making a Broadway debut, spun herself around, her arms outstretched. "New? In here? Not very likely!"

He, too, began laughing at the absurdity of the comment. Then he added, "Well, new for me. I've read one too many thrillers lately and want to try something else."

"How intriguing," she said. "Most people don't venture up here. Certainly not for that reason. Most people are looking for something in particular, or they are on a research project from the university. We don't get many casual readers up here."

David could feel his cheeks heating up, the color no doubt reddening as he realized the absurdity of it all.

"You're right. I'll head back down."

"No!" she said, a little too loudly, as she covered her mouth with her hands as if she herself was surprised at the volume. "I mean, it's a wonderful idea. You should, um, here, there's a little table and chair in the back corner. Why don't you explore for a while? I'll be back shortly. I just have to check on the other customers."

With that, she headed down the stairs and was gone.

David looked around the room. He was taking in all of the books, looking at their titles. There were no dust jackets, just beautifully bound books. He picked one up, blew the dust off it, and noticed the binding, the gold glimmer, the way the pages felt, heavier than today's paper. After reading a few paragraphs, he put it down and continued.

He noticed the book that the owner had been cleaning. It was hard to miss since it was the only one that was perfectly clean. He picked it up and flipped it open. An old paper fell to the floor. It was yellowed, and the way it had fallen to the ground immediately reminded him of the papers that had fallen in the park. He smiled again, remembering her, and thinking to himself how close he had been to seeing her again. In his mind, he rehearsed a conversation that ended with casually asking if she was free for dinner. He shook the thoughts from his mind and stooped down for the single page.

He picked it up and noticed the script, handwritten with flowing letters. He couldn't make out the words. He walked over to the little table in the corner and pulled the chain on the lamp. The green glass lampshade glowed.

At that very moment, he heard footsteps on the stairs. For a minute, he actually thought of putting the page in his pocket, but then thought better of it. The lady returned as she had said she would.

"What do you have there?" she asked, a curious look on her face.

"Oh, it fell out of that book," David said, his finger pointing to the book he had left on the shelf.

Her eyes widened. "What does it say?"

"Actually, I don't know. I just walked over to make it out in the light."

She crossed the room and joined him.

They both peered down, and David read the first words. "'Don't let them fall into enemy hands. But it's more than . . .'"

David stopped. His eyes squinted. "I can't make it out."

The Bookseller took the paper in her hands. She rocked the paper under the light, willing the writing to speak to her. "'All of it is based on belief, on empowerment, on purpose. No matter what happens, keep sharing the message of this book. And do not let it fall into enemy hands. Our existence is based...' "

She now struggled to see more.

"It's signed. I can make out an A. And I think it ends with an A, too," said David, his eyes trying to decipher more of the writing.

"That young woman who was just in here would be interested in this. We were just looking at the book together moments ago. It was one I purchased at an estate sale. Turns out, the estate was of her grandfather, and she was looking for it."

"You say she was just here? Who is she?" asked David, his question laced with a sense of surprise, and of hope, that the same young woman he saw leaving, the one from the park, was now within reach.

"I don't know more than that. She didn't say."

As the Bookseller said this, David's face dropped, disappointed. Sensing this, she added, "But I know she'll be back. She said as much."

She winked as she said this, and David felt his cheeks flush again.

"I'm going to save this for her, next time she is in. It may even have come from her family."

The Bookseller settled in a chair by the little table and motioned for David to sit down across from her. David took a deep breath, willing his heart to slow.

She tried again to make out the other words. "Maybe if we look with a magnifying glass. But I'll try that later. Let's go back to the beginning. When you first came in, you said you were looking to read something new. That's good," she said. "So often we get into patterns. Those patterns can be comforting. But staying in a comfortable pattern limits us. You know what I've noticed? Winners actually seek out the uncomfortable. Leaders consistently push beyond what's comfortable to stretch to new levels of achievement."

She said it with a strange tone, and David looked at her curiously. He studied her in the light and noticed her reaching for a book at her side. It looked like most of the books in the room. She opened it, and said in a matter-of-fact voice, "Mistake number five is staying in your comfort zone." The Bookseller looked up at him, a sly smile turning up her lips.

He should have seen this coming. It was there in the open, but he was so taken by the sight of the woman from the park and the letter that he missed the obvious clues.

"We fight against the pull of the mediocre. Mediocrity is the end result of too much comfort. All growth requires discomfort."

David's head was spinning. He was trying to listen to her. By this time in his journey, he had become a good listener, but it was a challenge now. He couldn't stop thinking about the young woman, the book, and even the earlier feeling that he was being watched. He willed himself to pay attention to the Bookseller, who was talking despite his wandering mind.

"Many successful authors have spoken at this store. One common theme I hear many of them talk about is the willingness to take risks, to fail, and yet to keep going. Nothing worthwhile is easy and comfortable. One famous journalist was here talking about his autobiography. He was constantly on the go, in dangerous places, reporting from around the world. He talked about this very thing, about being comfortable with the uncomfortable. He said that he may love to sit in his favorite chair at home, but nothing great would come from that. I will never forget something else he said . . ."

She looked at David, smiled, and said, "Let's take a walk. You need some air." With that, she made her way down the staircase and through the bookstore. The two of them were in the cool air outside a minute later. The light breeze felt great, and it jolted David back to himself.

"I'm sorry if I was fading," he said, looking to her for some type of approval.

"It's okay. A lot happened. But I do want you to get this one. It's a common trap for many people."

"You were saying something about an author or journalist?" asked David, hoping to impress her that he at least recalled where they were in the conversation.

"Yes, I was," she said. "He said that you have to be willing to try new things. As you get older, you feel funny about that, you want to look good, to be confident. But successful people are open about what they don't know. They're more willing to put themselves in situations where they admit that they are learning. And that is not just the key to learning new things, but to creating a great future."

She looked at David, who was now focused, the fresh air doing him some good. She continued. "Our thoughts can empower or imprison. They empower when we try something new, and they imprison when we let them convince us to stay comfortable."

The Bookseller looked directly into his eyes and said, "David, you're tired. Let's stop here. I'm sure to see you soon!" She tucked a paper into his hands, turned, and headed back the way they came. He was left standing there, weakly waving to her, trying to absorb the lessons of the fifth mistake while multiple questions circled him. He tucked the paper into his pocket without a glance and began to walk home. This time, he was walking more slowly, as if weighed down by it all.

MISTAKE #5:
Staying in Your Comfort Zone

Winners seek out the uncomfortable.

Leaders consistently push beyond what's comfortable to stretch to new levels of achievement.

Mediocrity is the end result of too much comfort.

The journey to success requires both risk and failure.

Growth happens with discomfort.

Success is the result of consistently and purposely doing the uncomfortable.

Our thoughts can empower or imprison.

MISTAKE SIX

It was now the dead of winter. It was far too cold for David to walk to work through the park. He was up early these days, hitting the gym first thing, focused on his goals. He was full of energy, brimming with enthusiasm. Life seemed good. After his very early workout, he was having breakfast with his new Success Mastermind Group.

They were a group of like-minded, driven business leaders who wanted to network and share what they were learning. After hearing about mistake number four and the need to find positive people, David decided to form the group. It was something he never would have done before. He remembered crafting the invitation and sending it to just four people. He didn't know them well, but knew they were driven, positive, and friendly. He shared his vision of a group, no more than twelve, to share ideas and challenge one another. Two of them said yes, and they met that first week. Their first order of business was creating a list of qualities for people they would recruit to their group. After a few months, the group had grown and fallen into a rhythm. Looking back, he realized even his small actions were driving him in a new, more positive direction. Now that he attended the weekly gatherings, he couldn't imagine starting a week without it.

Every week, someone led the discussion. They usually started with something positive that he or she had read that week and how it applied to something. What he really enjoyed about the group was the problem discussion. One or two of them would share a challenge, perhaps a difficult upcoming conversation, or advice on how to navigate a thorny issue. Hearing different perspectives and approaches was always enlightening. In fact, David used that advice throughout the week on unrelated issues. He had always avoided confrontation, and now, though he didn't wish it, he didn't shy away from it, either. All because of the group, pushing him out of his comfort zone to do and say things that he couldn't have imagined only a few months ago.

He was seriously working on his associates, his friends, who he was with on a daily basis. Before learning of the mistakes, he simply accepted the people who crossed his path. He wasn't intentional about his friends. Now, he was as careful selecting his friends as a coach is about selecting a winning team. And, though he couldn't change his relatives, he also steered conversations more easily and backed away when it seemed to be a never-ending drain on his energy. David didn't know whether others learned mistakes four and five together or not, but he could see that the two worked well for him. His positive friends were helping him do things he would never have done without their support.

Leaving the restaurant, David headed in to his job. Instead of just getting through the day, he was focused on what he could learn from the day. Everyone who crossed his path was a potential source of wisdom. After meeting so many people willing to share the mistakes, he began to realize that everyone had something they could teach him—even if it was what *not* to do.

It was strange, but after deciding that he would leave his job, he found things changing. Instead of constant worry, he was focused on preparing to launch his own business. That seemed to release his fear and allowed him to focus on the positive. He was building relationships for the future and learning everything he could. At the same time, he was considering other organizations where he could still continue to build toward his ultimate entrepreneurial goal. Which path was best for him was not clear yet.

One of the more recent assignments he had at work was to select the best marketing agency he could find. David's employer was rolling out a new product line, and it was his job to oversee the introduction by working with a marketing firm. He was more than excited.

Listening to different firms pitch their services was fascinating. He was taking copious and detailed notes. It was going to be difficult to choose, because all of them had something to offer.

And then one of the firms did something that stuck out. They brought along someone who had recently used their services. Instead of an endorsement or a list of references, this firm wanted him to meet a happy customer.

At one level, he was impressed with the story; but on another, he was intrigued. The Entrepreneur walked in, relaxed, confident, and with a big smile. He was happy with the marketing firm and how they were able to position his story. He showed David the sales figures, and they were well into the millions. He then switched to a more humble mode and shared the figures from his last few ventures.

"I had several products that failed, and I was this close to bank-ruptcy," he said emphasizing his point by squeezing his two fingers close together.

"I'm here because I feel I owe them," the Entrepreneur said, adding, "We disagreed on approach. We disagreed on position-ing. We disagreed on language." The right half of his face signaled a coming laugh before he broke into a full-fledged chuckle. "If we had done it my way, we would have sold maybe two units, instead of thousands."

The marketing firm's owner, now uncomfortable with all the praise, turned it back onto him and his product. "Thank you, but you had more than a little to do with your success. Still, I'm glad you were happy with what we did. Thank you so much for sharing your story."

The Entrepreneur dropped his business card on the conference room table and then said he was on his way to another meeting.

After the meeting ended, David couldn't stop thinking about the Entrepreneur's success story. There was something there that he couldn't quite put his finger on.

Later in the week, he called the number on the card and left a message. He didn't normally do that, and David was sure the Entrepreneur was busy and really had no reason to return the call. He doubted he would hear anything more.

Two hours later, the Entrepreneur was on the phone, agreeing to lunch. "I'm glad you called, because I was going to call you if you didn't reach out," he said.

Disconnecting the call, David wondered about that last comment.

Monday came, and David arrived early at the restaurant for lunch. The Entrepreneur was already at the far end of the restaurant scribbling something down and sipping an iced tea. David crossed the dining room and extended his hand.

"Thank you for agreeing to see me," David started. "I was so taken by your story, not just the success, but also the failure. The way you talked about it was...different."

The Entrepreneur nodded as the server dropped off menus, explained specials, and welcomed them. After ordering, the two resumed the conversation.

"Tell me more about why this product took off when the others didn't," David said. "Oh, one more thing. We already picked the firm. Your friends won, so I'm really more interested about this personally than professionally."

"I heard that," the Entrepreneur said, adding, "and I think you'll be very happy with your decision."

The Entrepreneur was relaxed and somewhat pensive for a moment. "I have tried so many things. I tried selling one product; it was taking off, but I didn't have enough inventory and no cash to buy more. By the time I had stock, a competitor had a cheaper and, I guess, a better version."

At that moment, the food arrived at the table. Not expecting anything in particular, David was pleasantly surprised by the presentation, by the taste, by the entire meal. It was unusually good, a place he would be returning to. He had to prompt the Entrepreneur back into the conversation. "You were telling me about running out of inventory."

"Yes, that did happen, but the point is really that anything can happen out there. It's what happens in here," he said, tapping his right temple, before continuing, "that determines your success."

The two ate in companionable silence for a bit, and then the

Entrepreneur pushed his empty plate away as he continued talking. "Another time, I started a service where I made a margin off all the products sold through my website. It really took off. Then I got into a big intellectual property dispute with another company. I didn't have the money to fight back, so we folded."

David was listening. He could see how open the Entrepreneur was in sharing his wins and his losses. It was refreshing not to hear a prepackaged story where everything was somehow perfect. They enjoyed a long conversation, and the Entrepreneur was talking about how he messed things up or how things didn't work out.

"At first, I would blame everything and everybody. It was his fault. It was her mistake. It was that the bank fees were too high. Or taxes were eating into our profits. It was that prices were too high or I couldn't get enough good workers. On and on. And then I realized that all of those things were not going to change. All of that stays the same. And it's the same for everybody. I had to change. I had to change my thinking."

The Entrepreneur's attention drifted far away again. It was at least a minute before he said, "Excuses are the weeds that choke progress. Setbacks are the seeds that sprout opportunity. Now my thinking is different. When I start to blame someone or something, I stop myself and adjust my thinking. And then, when something goes wrong, I realize it simply means I am edging closer to success."

As he spoke, David immediately thought about mistake number three and accepting excuses. The Entrepreneur clearly was a master of personal accountability.

"Now...tell me about you," the Entrepreneur said. "Are you thinking of starting something new?"

"I like my job," David said, "well, compared to a few months ago, anyway. I am thinking about eventually starting my own firm.

Right now things are going well enough, I suppose. At least I'm not worried about getting fired these days."

The Entrepreneur turned very serious and said, "Don't let current circumstances define your destiny, whether good or bad. You have to go for what's in your heart. In every profession, in every venture, in every life there is failure. Some people run from it. Some people ignore it. Some people pretend it didn't happen. But I have never met a successful person who couldn't talk about failing."

Nodding his head, David agreed. "It seems that the bigger the success, the more open people are to talk about failing, because they no longer resent that part."

"I see your point," the Entrepreneur said. "Successful people don't really look at it as failure. We look at it as a setback, as part of the plan. It may even be a stepping-stone."

"One of the biggest mistakes people make in life..." The Entrepreneur paused, and then reached into the bag he had at his feet.

"I've been wondering if you would pull out that old book ever since you started talking so openly about making excuses," David said.

Smiling, the Entrepreneur said, "Excuses. I talk about it because that was the big one for me. And this one is related. Mistake number six is allowing temporary setbacks to become permanent failures."

He let the words sink in, hanging in the air between them, not saying anything else.

Before David interrupted the silence, the Entrepreneur continued his explanation. "Some people take a shot, miss, and give up. They give a speech, bomb, and never get in front of a room again. Maybe they lose money on an investment and think, 'No way can I handle money.' It's awful.

"That type of thinking cements. It hardens, strengthens, and is difficult to break through. If we quickly get back into the game, step back to the podium, make another investment, we remold ourselves before our failure has time to dry. And we turn it into something else. At the end of the year, we may look back and see that one event as a mistake, but it's a blip on the way to something more. All of it starts with how we think. Positive expectation is how it begins."

"I think I get it," David said, reflecting on all that was said. "I have let that thinking cement. When I was a teenager, I worked in a sales job. It was awful. I couldn't sell a thing and have run away from sales ever since. I guess I need to change that thinking and expect more."

"Exactly. A setback is compounded when you allow an unwelcome label to stick. Don't accept a temporary experience as a permanent declaration. It doesn't mean you have to be good at everything or do everything, but if you think it's a skill that you need to fulfill your purpose, you need to find a way through it."

The two of them stood up, shook hands, and started to leave the restaurant. David ran back to the table, looking for something. Seeing nothing, he exited the front door and saw the Entrepreneur standing on the front step.

"Looking for this?" he asked with a sheepish grin. Handing him a paper, he said, "Good luck on this journey. It's an extraordinary opportunity if you make the most of it."

The two shook hands in farewell and parted ways. At home, David read the paper again. As he did, he replayed the conversation with the Entrepreneur. There were so many lessons, but it wasn't just the wisdom. It was the way the Entrepreneur was so genuine and open about it all. He resolved not to forget his attitude.

MISTAKE #6:
Allowing Temporary Setbacks to Become Permanent Failures

Quickly getting back into the game remolds our experience positively before it has time to harden negatively.

Your thoughts control your destiny.

Don't get through the day; learn from the day.

Don't let current circumstances define your destiny.

A setback is compounded when you allow an unwelcome label to stick.

Setbacks are the seeds that sprout opportunity.

Excuses are the weeds that try to choke progress.

Don't accept a temporary experience as a permanent declaration.

Look at everyone you meet as a wise teacher.

Successful people see temporary failures as stepping-stones to success.

THE SECOND LAW

⌘⌘⌘

Aria stood in the rain, a stinging, drenching pour that made her think of God and the angels kicking over buckets in heaven. She didn't run. She remained perfectly still, letting it soak her body through her layers of clothing, hoping it would wash away the pain of loss. It had been a week since her uncle had died, and she still struggled to accept that he was gone. She barely remembered her parents; Uncle Raymond was the only father she knew, and now he was gone and she felt utterly alone in the world. How long she was there she didn't know, didn't really care. A break in the rain allowed the moonlight to spill out of the dark sky, suddenly illuminating the ground. Rivulets of water looked like broken crystal all the way from the barn to Robert and Mae's house.

In that moment, she allowed herself to cry, a real cry, one that welled up from deep inside. As she did, the clouds reopened, muffling her sobs.

What would she do without her beloved uncle? Today was the day she had dreaded for so long. She simply couldn't let go of him.

Her mind began replaying all of their conversations: the manuscript, the Teachers, the role of the Keeper, the mysteries of it all.

Tracing her way across the yard, she tried her best to avoid the mud, though she knew that, at this stage, it wouldn't matter much. She tucked her auburn hair behind her ears and then sat down on the front steps of the house. She had to think.

Her thoughts were jumbled, each surfacing as if to grab a breath before being pushed back under by yet another. Love, anger, despair: each emotion locked in a competition for her attention. Aria rested her face in her hands. Lightning once again lit up the sky, and thunder groaned in response. Searching for answers, she listened to the rain pound the ground all around her.

Finally, she stood up and groped in the dark for the doorknob. Her foot began to slide on the floor, and she caught herself from spilling over. She lit a candle and made her way to the guest room. She was so thankful that Robert and Mae had been there for her, welcoming her to stay as long as she needed. Her mind raced ahead while still trying to make sense of it all. Everything in her life was now upturned. Her uncle gone. Her home gone as well. Her new responsibility as Keeper. Protecting the manuscript. The Teachers. Not to mention Alexander's betrayal. And Ulrick.

She readied herself for bed and then lay there, staring in the dark, motionless.

Slowly, her shock and sadness began to give way to anger and resolve. Her emotions shifted with the storm outside, which faded so quickly it was as if the angels decided to put their toys away and themselves to bed.

The familiar night sounds returned but were not comforting this evening. Instead of putting her to sleep, it was as if a bug orchestra were signaling warnings of what was ahead, the crescendo of alarm deafening. How ironic that, for many months, she had wished the Teachers to appear, waiting in eager expectation of the next lesson. Now she wanted to turn back the clock and enjoy the moments of learning and slow it all down.

She lay awake most of the night, thinking, weighing her options, imagining the future. How different that future would be than the one she imagined only last week. Her uncle then still alive, her mission so different, her dream of a life with Alexander, one filled with children, with love, infused with the energy of purpose. She decided she had to leave it all behind, letting go of the past. She got back out of bed, slid her uncle's box from under the bed. Using the brass key, she opened it and rummaged for the papers. She held them to the moonlight and read the Second Law of the Keeper.

The Law of Gratitude

The Law of Gratitude is the second law. Gratitude is the fertilizer for the bounty of success, the enabler of the harvest. A grateful spirit magnetizes people, ideas, and opportunity.

With a grateful heart one is able to receive blessings that pass over those who are bitter. Uplifted hands of gratitude have no expectation and yet are filled joyfully with abundance.

Inside a thankful person is love and an overflow of joy. One may unlock the mystery inside with a continually thankful attitude. Those who drink richly from the cup of thankfulness find themselves refreshed and their cup refilled. Count your daily blessings until your years are rich.

On its wings, gratitude lifts those in despair onto winds of plenty to fly above life's pains into the everlasting place of abundance. Speak gratitude to others and you fuel the mysterious power of the spirit.

Reading these words, Aria decided to think about the special people in her life and the opportunity she had ahead of her. Instead of thinking of all she had lost, she made a decision to be appreciative of the opportunity she had had to know her uncle, to learn from him, and to experience his presence.

Her uncle had never had a chance to explain to her why the Law of Gratitude was so important to the Keeper. She could imagine it used falsely, with wrong motives, and how and why it would be dangerous. Still, there was something else in the Second Law of the Keeper that she could not quite figure out, something beneath the words that she just could not place.

She let it go and said out loud the names of the people whom she was grateful to know, who had made a difference in her life.

Finally, Aria was able to still her mind enough to sleep. She dreamed of *The Book of Mistakes* and of finding the Third Law of the Keeper. Her uncle died without revealing its location, leaving her searching. His last words to her echoed in her mind. She was to seek inside. Her mind wrestled with the responsibility of finding the last law and protecting the manuscript.

She woke up the next morning and dressed with a rhythm, an internal beat prodding her along. An hour later, she was on a horse and heading into town to visit her uncle Raymond's office.

She tied the horse in front of the office and walked up the slabs of stone to the front door. Her mind was still on the Second Law and her heart stopped when she looked up. Ulrick, Alexander, and three other men were standing in front of the office.

What now?

"Aria, I've been worried about you," Alexander said. "I'm so sorry for your loss." His eyes, full of compassion, seemed so sincere.

"We all are," Ulrick said. "I knew your uncle well." Alexander quickly made introductions.

Aria simply nodded, revealing little.

"In addition to offering our deepest sympathies," Ulrick said, in a voice with poorly disguised loathing, "we hoped to discuss a vital matter with you. I believe your uncle had something that is dear to me."

Aria swallowed and tried to compose herself and hide her true feelings. "What would my uncle possibly have that would interest you?" She looked up, directly into Ulrick's eyes. She felt the coldness in them, the darkness. She couldn't look at him for long and glanced away, over to Alexander. When they locked eyes, she looked away again, blushing and confused. Why Alexander worked for a man like this was not something she understood.

"I went to the reading of his last will and testament. In it, your uncle declared that he was giving you his library, his books, and some manuscripts. I want to make a claim on one, as I believe it was wrongfully given to him and belongs rightfully to my family."

Aria tried not to stifle a laugh, knowing how ridiculous this false claim was. "I'm afraid that most of those are gone. Did you hear that our family home burned to the ground?"

"No, I didn't," Ulrick lied, as easily as he breathed. "But surely he kept many of them here as well. We just want to look around. Let's see what's inside."

Inside? Aria thought back to the Second Law, the words coming back to her mind. *Inside. Inside.* And her uncle's last words. *Inside.* It was like a revelation to her as she realized she needed to get back to Robert and Mae's home, but not before delaying Ulrick and the men here.

Alexander's voice cut through the silence. "Aria, I was there the night of the fire. I saw your home burn to the ground. I'm sorry."

His admission caught Aria by surprise, igniting a small spark of hope.

He continued. "That night, I heard such a commotion of voices that I woke up. Someone in our house had seen the smoke in the distance and raised the alarm. I headed immediately to your home. I was so relieved to learn you were away at the time. That you were safe. I've been trying to talk with you ever since."

Aria looked at him, wanting to wash everything away and return to the way it was days ago when she had complete trust in him. Now he was pulling her heartstrings one way while doubts clawed in the opposite direction. She quickly closed her eyes, composed herself, and thought of a plan that would allow her the opportunity she needed. They didn't know what she knew, and she would not allow her heart's weakness, Alexander, to muddy her mission.

"I'm so glad to see you, Alexander. Please do come in, all of you," Aria said, stepping up to the door and unlocking it. She felt like she was betraying her uncle by letting them in, but she felt that this confrontation was inevitable. Better they come in and look in the light of day than breaking in by night and damaging something. This way she could be somewhat in control of it, too, she thought.

"If there is something that rightfully belongs to your family, I'm sure my uncle would want it returned," she said, leading the way.

Inside the office, she pointed them to the shelves and told them to get started. She slipped into another room, found an empty box, and filled it with papers. She hoped that when they found this, it would delay and confuse them just long enough for her plan to work. If they somehow thought this was the manuscript, it would change their focus for a while.

"Don't let me distract you from your search," Aria said when she returned to the room. "I will be down the hall going through some of his things. This is a very difficult time for me."

With that, Aria slipped back out the front door, completely unnoticed. She was back on her horse and pushing fast to return to the guest room. She hoped that her mind had truly given her the answer to the mysterious location of the Third Law.

⌘⌘⌘

MISTAKE SEVEN

The sun was so bright and warm, David felt it surround him long before he opened his eyes. How long he had slept, he didn't know, and didn't care. He felt free, in a way he hadn't in a long time.

Last night, he had driven up to visit his parents in the country. After an incredible home-cooked dinner and a conversation that lasted well into the early hours, he collapsed into the newly redecorated guest bedroom. It felt like a bed and breakfast, with decorative touches that hinted at both sexes so that it wasn't overly feminine, nor masculine, just cozy, like a warm hug. He knew he would sleep well, and he did.

No longer was he afraid of losing his job or of running out of money or of ruining his reputation. He wasn't pursuing status or fame. He was infinitely comfortable, calm in a way that was hard to articulate. He knew that this newfound peace was because of the teachers, pushing him to work on himself, avoid the mistakes, and pursue a life of excellence. Strangely, even though he felt this calmness, he was still driving toward his goals. One of the people in his mastermind group made an observation that echoed in his mind:

success is when you're filled with ambition and peace in equal measure at the same time.

Lying in bed, not yet fully awake, he could hear the faint notes of a piano downstairs. Thoughts of the past week flashed through his mind. He recalled the second interview he'd recently had with a new company that he really thought would land him an offer. It seemed a great fit for him, one where he would use his creative talents and still build toward his ultimate goal of starting a firm. But, instead of the call with an offer, he received a polite note explaining that someone else was a better fit. *You'll never get a job in a company like that. It would be too perfect.* The thought was there, fueling his doubts, and he willed it away. One of his new friends said that she would accept the thought and then replace it. *When the right opportunity presents itself, nothing will stop me from it.* He repeated it several times in his semi-awake, semi-sleeping state. *A temporary setback is only a setup for a permanent step forward.*

The piano began to crescendo, and David stirred in bed. His mom had told him to expect visitors this morning, including someone he was looking forward to seeing. More than a musician, he was also the city's celebrated Conductor. He and his wife were dear friends of the family, and they were enjoying a weekend outside the hurried pace of the city.

The Conductor was actually more of a friend to David than to his parents. Years ago, the Conductor doubled as the local orchestra and band director, and David had found himself in his classes for years. During those classes, and after, David learned more about life than about music. The Conductor was full of surprises, and his positive spirit likely did more to encourage David's drive than he had imagined.

Not yet opening his eyes, David listened again for the faint sounds of the baby grand piano. His mind was reaching out through the distance from his bedroom to the living room in an effort to discern the chosen piece. At that moment, the tempo switched to a lively pace.

"Of course," David said, realizing, "Beethoven. Sonata Pathétique."

It was an interesting choice, and David knew that the Conductor was always clever in his decisions. He remembered the history from his class. Beethoven was only twenty-seven when he wrote the piece, and dedicated it to a friend, a prince, he recalled, though the name escaped him. The piece sold well at the time for Beethoven and helped secure his reputation. It marked a small turning point for him, a message not lost on David.

Was the Conductor signaling that he had also made a turning point?

I wouldn't put it past him, thought David. As he opened his eyes, he took in the brightness of the room and the nearly blinding light of the reflected sun in the mirror across from the large bed.

He was up, brushing his teeth, fixing his hair, and downstairs in no time. It was 9:30 a.m. as he slipped into the living room. By this time, the Conductor was laughing with the family while simultaneously playing Gershwin, almost as a background piece.

"It's not every day I can sleep in and wake up to extraordinary classical sounds played live by my friend."

The Conductor smiled. "Good morning! So good to see you again."

He looked both the same and different. The same fire in his eyes, in his expression, but perhaps slightly weaker, his posture bent a bit forward, his fingers slightly gnarled with arthritis. But his playing was near perfection, and he didn't even consider himself a musician.

After excusing himself to get some coffee and a bagel, David entered the kitchen, which had not yet been redone like most of the house. His mother couldn't wait for its remodel, but his father was slowing this part of the project because of the disruption it would cause.

The Conductor had stopped playing the piano. David could hear laughing and the grating of the piano bench on the wood floor as it was slid back. The Conductor appeared in the kitchen.

"May I join you for a second cup?" he asked. As they settled down at the kitchen table, which was really a half-booth with a bench on one side and three chairs on the other, the music started again. David wasn't surprised. The Conductor's wife was equally accomplished in her musical ability and had replaced him at the piano, no doubt at his mother's request. As long as trained pros were in the house, you could be sure she would be coaxing them to continue. If they even so much as paused, her face would fall dramatically in such a way that they would immediately pick it back up. If you watched his mother's face, it was almost as if she was singing each piano note internally, her own private opera. And, every once in a while, a great show tune would cause her to burst into song without reservation and really without her even realizing she was doing it.

David was thrilled to spend some uninterrupted time with his mentor. He guessed that they would start with music, turn to politics, then to the personal. He was only slightly off when the first question was about a local political race. The two were on opposite sides of the political spectrum, but, unlike most people who disagreed, they actually delighted in arguing back and forth about substance, about perceptions, and about what was best for the future. It was just like old times.

The subject shifted, naturally, from politics to life.

"How have you been?" the Conductor asked, the simple question lobbed across the table. But the Conductor was not one for small talk. The question was laced with deeper meaning, a reconnaissance question probing into unknown territory.

"I have been through a lot, learned a lot. The working world wasn't exactly what I expected. The politics, the people. It's been eye-opening. But some amazing things have happened to me. I don't think I could explain. Actually, I don't think you'd even believe me," David said, his eyes deliberately widening on the last sentence.

"Try me?" asked the Conductor, but, before waiting to hear an explanation, he added, "Why do you think Mozart was such a phenomenon?"

It was not unlike the Conductor to do this, shifting the conversation back to his favorite subject of music and its history. And David always went along, realizing that the ebb and flow of the conversation would return naturally.

"He was never satisfied," the Conductor said, answering his own question. "He was always pushing, always doing something new. Look at almost any point of his career and he could have stayed there, but he was ambitious, wanted to keep going. He refused to fit in to the expectations of the day. He refused to be categorized. He wanted to be remembered. He wanted to create masterpieces!"

David waited a beat, looking for the hook back from Mozart to his own story. The Conductor offered nothing, but continued his history lesson moments later.

"He realized he needed to keep learning. When symphony wasn't enough, he moved to opera, to chamber music, to comedy. You name it, he would take it on."

David loved to hear the Conductor teach. He might have been

a renowned Conductor, celebrated for his skill, but he remained a teacher at heart.

David thought he had it down by now, thought he knew when to expect it, thought he knew what would happen. But this time he was taken completely off guard. He hadn't been this surprised since the very beginning of the strange events that had unfolded in his life.

Because, at that very moment, with not the least bit of fanfare, the Conductor reached down to his side and picked up the ancient book, the one that had dazzled David for months, and read some words.

"Mistake number seven is blending in instead of standing out."

"I don't know what to say," stammered David, though the Conductor was clearly enjoying the element of surprise. "Really. One of the teachers of the mistakes was, well, one of my teachers!"

The Conductor waved him off and continued on as if this happened every day of his life. "Mozart worked feverishly. His work ethic was tireless and matched by his drive to succeed. His influence remains unparalleled to this very day.

"Think of this. He wrote six hundred pieces before he died. And he died at thirty-five!"

"That sounds younger every day," said David in response, trying to elicit a smile.

"That's just a kid!" responded the Conductor, adding, "Forget classical music for a second. Just think about anyone having this type of lasting impact on the world so quickly." The Conductor emphasized the word "lasting" in the way only he could, holding up a hand and drawing out a note as if he was in his tuxedo on stage leading a rehearsal.

"You are really enjoying this, aren't you?" inquired David, watching his mentor blend the mystery of the mistakes with his love of musical history.

"Most of us spend our lives learning to blend in. In the teenage years especially, we are picked on relentlessly if we dare to stand out."

As he said this, David recalled an incident when he was made fun of for days because of something he wore in the seventh grade. He nodded his head in agreement without saying anything.

"Most of us have such a powerful emotional connection to blending in that we don't even imagine a plan to stand out. But greatness always stands out. If you fail to stand out, you're passed over at promotion time. Overlooked in the marketplace. Ignored for the most important opportunities."

David was so relaxed this morning, in his childhood home, the sounds of the piano in the background, talking with his friend. He seemed to be taking this mistake in at a deeper level.

"Name three people that are mega-successful," the Conductor said. Before waiting for an answer, he added, "I am absolutely certain that they all stood out. It doesn't even have to be superstardom; think about someone who is really good at what she does." The Conductor paused, sipping his now cool cup of coffee as he looked at David. He was subtly checking in to see if he was still paying attention.

His star pupil hadn't missed a word.

The Conductor continued. "Standing out is as simple as consistently outperforming expectations."

David's brown eyes squinted involuntarily as the sun shifted and nudged through the clouds, brightening the room. "I can see that. I mean, even at work, the culture teaches you to fall in line, to not stand out, keep your head down and all of that."

"Most of us feel uncomfortable when someone doesn't blend in. There are powerful norms designed to keep people in line. You have to recognize that for what it is. Great leaders resist the pull of the normal and push through to the extraordinary."

At that moment, the music in the other room grew quiet. They must have decided to talk, but it was obvious they were giving the two old friends privacy. David appreciated the alone time. He traced his finger along the wood of the kitchen table, lost in thought, contemplating the lessons of this mistake.

"Here's what I found most powerful about this mistake," said the Conductor. "Authenticity is the result of standing out. If you are true to your design, you naturally stand out from others because no one else is quite like you. Authenticity is the beautiful expression of your unique giftedness."

The Conductor then closed the ancient book and folded it into his lap. Grabbing David's arm, he squeezed it and pushed himself up from the table.

"Of all of our talks, this one has been my very favorite," the Conductor said. "It was such a privilege to be the one to share this with you."

He placed the book carefully into a bag, nodded, and then added, "I'm going back in before they come looking for us. How about some Chopin now?"

David smiled, lost in his own thoughts, barely registering that his friend was walking back to join his family. Then he was up with a jolt, thinking that the Conductor had forgotten something critically important. Following the Conductor, he stopped and found what he was looking for on the kitchen counter. He hadn't noticed the Conductor placing it there, but it was as he expected. He read it slowly, knowing he would read its words many times in the coming days.

MISTAKE #7:
Trying to Blend In instead of Standing Out

Most of us spend our lives learning to blend in when success is about standing out.

Successful people are always pushing, always learning, always doing something new.

Greatness always stands out.

If you fail to stand out, you will be overlooked, passed over, and ignored.

Standing out is as simple as consistently outperforming expectations.

Great leaders resist the pull of the normal and push through to the extraordinary.

Authenticity is the result of standing out.

If you are true to your unique design, you naturally stand out.

Authenticity is the beautiful expression of your unique giftedness.

MISTAKE EIGHT

Colors exploded off the canvas. With each brushstroke, the Artist masterfully added another surprising element: a hint of green, a burst of red, mountains, a stream. The Artist methodically applied paint with a sense of purpose as if guided by an unseen plan. She was working unusually early this morning, enjoying the time between seasons. Not quite spring, but winter had lessened its grip.

Her studio was located on a busy street, and those rushing by could peer inside and glimpse her at work. Several stopped to watch, taken by her vigor and energy as she created explosions of color.

The early morning sun provided the perfect opportunity to showcase the painting's brilliance. The Artist didn't look up, didn't even realize that a crowd was growing outside her window. Admirers were pointing, talking about her talent.

David found himself on this street unexpectedly. The path through the park was closed, undergoing some repairs from winter's damaging storms. As he was earlier than usual, he stopped when he saw the crowd at the window. He recognized the style of the painting immediately. She was the creator of the spectacular painting he'd seen at the bank when he'd gone to ask for a loan.

Just when he looked in, the Artist looked up, glancing at the crowd and then settling her eyes directly on his. She paused, put down her brush with considerable care, and then went to the door. She opened the studio door and welcomed everyone inside. A few took that opportunity to head back on their way, but most of them did enter the studio and began browsing through the works for sale.

Approaching David, the Artist said, "Thank you for stopping in. I'm glad you're here. Would you like to see how I work?"

David responded, "I'm early for work and the crowd caught my attention. I'm certainly not in the market for high-end paintings, but I love watching your creativity."

The Artist smiled a genuine smile, one that radiated happiness, peace, and kindness all at once. David felt warmth and a welcoming spirit.

"Come back here and let me show you how it all happens," she said, motioning him to one side.

She continued the painting, but added commentary as she did. It reminded David of a television show he had watched long ago. An artist would talk to an imaginary audience as he painted landscapes, making it look simple, though most people watching wouldn't dare to try what he did.

Then she did something he didn't expect.

She picked up the brush, dipped it into a blended color, and handed it to David.

"Your turn," she said and, looking at him expectantly, added, "No better time than now."

"I'm sorry. I'm definitely on the creative side, but I don't have a painting bone in my body," David said.

"The world has unlimited opportunity. Our minds constrict us. Change the limitation in the mind and the restrictions are gone. Close your eyes and see what you want to create."

The Artist wrapped her hands around David's, and, as if she were a magician, the brush somehow landed in his grip. The next thing he knew his hand was guided to the painting. He was frozen in place, worried that anything he did would ruin what was clearly going to be an expensive painting.

Guiding him along, the Artist began to work seemingly through him.

"Don't worry about a mistake. We can fix anything." She continued with constant encouragement and, before he knew it, he was truly painting. He didn't know how or where it came from, but a few minutes later, he stepped back and was somewhat pleased with what he had added to the scene. He knew it would not have been possible without her guidance, but he was still smiling.

"Terrific work," the Artist said. "You have hidden talent."

"Thanks for letting me do that. I understand you may need to fix what I did." David looked at the scene on the canvas admiringly. He carefully handed her the brush, which she expertly cleaned and put away.

"I may touch it up and enhance it a bit, but you did good work!" the Artist said before turning to him and asking a question that caught him off guard. "If your life was a canvas, would you be pleased with what you are creating?"

David looked up and then glanced around the room. He was looking for something, his eyes searching. He wondered whether this was the next lesson, the next mistake. He decided to just ask directly. "You wouldn't happen to have a small leather book nearby with some powerful lessons in it, would you?"

The Artist gave a knowing laugh and said, "Why, now that you mention it..." She pulled the book off a nearby shelf. "I guess by the time you get to number eight, you're on the lookout."

"You could say that," David said. "But I didn't suspect it until that penetrating question. To answer it, I would say, not quite yet, but I feel like I am moving in a much better direction."

"That's an honest answer," the Artist said. "We often hear that life is a gift. That's true, but it is not a gift to put on a shelf and admire. It's a gift to create! We can create anything we choose. We design it, and that design starts in our thinking. I imagine something until it is so clear in my mind that it transfers onto the canvas seamlessly. In fact, anything we repeatedly imagine with intensity creates it. I'm not just an Artist in the traditional sense, either, you should know," she said, before picking up another book and showing it to him. It was filled with numbers and spreadsheets.

"My business is successful not only for the art I sell here. I also have a line of designer cards, a clothing line, and on and on. It's a growing enterprise. But I almost messed it all up. It was mistake number eight that made the most difference in my life."

"That's extraordinary. I had no idea you had so many products related to your art. Incredible. Please don't make me wait any longer. What is mistake eight?"

"Mistake number eight is thinking that there is a fixed and limited amount of success available."

Right after she said that, one of her employees waved her over. One of the customers was nearly begging for a personalized signature. The Artist excused herself and left to attend to her newest fan. David watched her walk over and connect with someone as she signed the painting. Returning to David, she continued as if she had never left. "When I was starting, I would see what someone else had done. I became jealous. I would compare myself to them. If they were doing well, I would burn inside. I couldn't explain it, and it's embarrassing, but it's true."

David thought about his successful, "semi-famous" friend who was regularly in the news and nodded. "Believe me, I understand," he said.

She was candid if nothing else, and David appreciated that each person sharing the mistakes was so open about what their own mistakes were.

"If someone was doing well, I guess I thought it meant less for me. I had yet to realize this: There is unlimited possibility in the universe. There is no limit to your potential. Someone else's success does not reduce your own capabilities or potential. Be motivated, not intimidated, by another's success."

David posed a series of rapid-fire questions to her. "How do you develop that mindset? Is it always true? Why doesn't this thinking feel natural to me?" His curiosity and desire to understand the power of this mistake grew as he thought about its implications.

The Artist acknowledged his questions with a nod and a smile. Her finger signaled that she would return to his inquiries. She didn't answer them directly, but continued. "If someone sold an expensive painting at a show, I thought, 'Oh, great, that was likely the only buyer at that price point.' It made me mad. It wasn't until later that I realized there are an unlimited number of ways to be successful. The only limitations that I need to worry about are the ones in my mind."

David said, "You have such a successful business, I'm surprised you even remember what it was like to start out."

"Oh, I do. I replay it all the time—in a positive way—to remind myself what really matters and how to help others. And you know what? When I started having some success, I would look down at a struggling artist, and I guess I felt pretty good. That was pride. It was ugly. I had to work hard on that. Successful people look at others on the same path and show the way, encouraging them to reach higher. The more you help others, the more you attract success. It's amazing."

The Artist wanted to make a point, so she paused and offered David a chance to sit down. They sat at a small table in the corner of the studio. One of the Artist's employees appeared with two piping hot cups of coffee. She said, "I want to say this again because it's so important. There is unlimited opportunity. When someone else succeeds, watch your mindset. Turn jealousy and envy into curiosity."

David thought about turning envy into curiosity. Instead of being jealous of his most successful friend, he should have quizzed him about all aspects of his success and learned how and why it happened for him. Had he done that, he might have found some clues for his own journey.

The Artist sensed he was deep in thought, so she waited an appropriate time and then continued. "When someone is successful, or happy, or peaceful, ask why. You'll be surprised at how open that person will be, and many times you'll find an obvious road map for your own use. If it fits your purpose, design it into your plans."

The two continued to talk for some time before the Artist again left to sign another painting. David thought about his feelings toward others who were doing well and even about someone who had graduated with him who wasn't doing so well. He decided right then to call his friend who was struggling and offer a helping hand. And then he sent a message to someone who was doing so well that she was hitting it out of the park. He asked if they could get together so David could learn from her. Not a minute later, she responded that she would be happy to.

When the Artist returned, David shared this with her, finished his coffee, and stood up to leave. The Artist hugged David and offered some encouraging words. Then she stopped herself. "I should also add that it works in reverse. If someone has failed, is miserably unhappy, agitated all the time, stressed to a boiling point, ask and ask. They, too, were on a journey, but slipped somehow into a trap. These lessons, what *not* to do, are often just as important as what *to* do!"

She then took a paper and tucked it into his jacket pocket. David asked, "You're not even trying the subterfuge to sneak it in?"

The Artist laughed and said, "I think you know how this works by now."

David didn't leave right away. Instead, he watched her from a distance. How she interacted with people, how she made everyone welcome. Each person clearly felt as if he was the most important person in the shop. He was particularly impressed when he saw her with a small child, a little girl who had brought in her own painting to show to her. By the way she reacted, you would have thought that a baby Monet or Picasso was in the store.

Finally, David gave a friendly wave to the Artist. She waved back. As he exited the gallery, one of the employees stopped him. "She wanted you to have this." He reached out and accepted a small, carefully wrapped package.

David then crossed the street and thought about the lessons from the Artist. When he arrived at his office, he unwrapped the package and found a beautiful painting of a park on a fall day.

Immediately, he did a double take. It was not any park, but *the* park. Complete with the bench, the tree, and even the beautiful girl. That very first day, the one that started it all seemed captured in the painting. This was too much. "Impossible," he said to himself.

He decided to stop back and visit the Artist again and ask about it. David then pulled out the paper and read.

MISTAKE #8:
Thinking That There Is a Fixed and Limited Amount of Success Available

Our thinking determines the design of our life.

Anything we repeatedly imagine with intensity becomes reality.

There is unlimited possibility in the universe.

There is no limit to your potential.

The only limitations you need to worry about are the ones in your mind.

Be motivated, not intimidated, by another's success.

Successful people help others through encouragement and experience.

Helping others magnetizes people to your cause and enhances your success.

When someone is doing well, change your mindset from jealousy to curiosity.

⌘⌘⌘

Arriving at Robert and Mae's home, Aria ran up the front stairs and pulled the heavy door. It swung open, and she called out a greeting. The door closed behind her, and she saw Mae leaning out into the hallway, welcoming her. Aria waved back and immediately headed to her room.

After closing her door, she looked out the window to ensure she had no visitors behind her. The clouds were thick, darkening and covering the sun. She saw no one.

She moved to the edge of her bed and sunk down on one knee. Her right hand reached under the bed and probed for the small chest. Her hand felt the ring on top, and she pulled it out carefully. Taking another precaution, she got up and went back to the door of room. She pulled the room's chair over and underneath the doorknob.

A second later, she pulled open the box and carefully lifted out the manuscript of *The Book of Mistakes*. She checked to be sure that the last page was as she left it, and it was: the Second Law of the Keeper now immediately behind the first. She scanned it and saw the words "inside" in the law in a new light. Her uncle's last words came to her.

She felt the bottom of the box. Nothing.

She traced the edge with her fingernail. A string. Or more like a few threads. She twisted them between two fingers and then gently tugged. It lifted up, revealing a false bottom.

There it was. The Third Law of the Keeper. Not to mention some rather beautiful gold coins carefully lining the true bottom of the box.

She wanted to read the Third Law, but something made her pause. She stopped. Her mind realized that she now had the entire manuscript of the Keeper and that she must keep it safe. She tucked everything back into the box.

She had to disappear with the box, and fast. She knew Ulrick would stop at nothing, and she wanted to secure the manuscript far away from him.

Aria got up and went back to the window. Still no one.

So why didn't she have any comfort?

She went over to the corner of the room and found her uncle's satchel. She put the box in the satchel and some limited number of things she would need. She realized that he must have carried it often in the same manner.

She glanced around the room. She remembered her uncle had left some money for her, and she retrieved that as well. And then she slipped back out the front door, unnoticed, carrying the satchel on her shoulder.

A steady rain beat against her cloak as she made her way across the field. It was only a degree or two north of freezing, and Aria felt the chill clawing at her. What kept her going was the thought of the men seeking her, knowing that they would steal the manuscript and likely force the secrets from her mind. At the far end of the field, she stopped. She slipped into a prone position in the mud to avoid any detection.

There they were. The men must have realized she had evaded them. She could see Ulrick leading them in front, riding a pale gray horse. Alexander was in the middle of the group. She wanted to put as much distance as possible between herself and them. Aria kept her eye on Ulrick as he approached the front of the house. She knew Mae would answer and that she would also think she was home. Her horse was in plain view, furthering the illusion that she was present. That gave her some more time as long as they didn't look in her direction.

She moved stealthily, inching backward until she was behind some tall bushes and protected from view. She kept a steady pace but was careful to maintain near silence as she moved.

Approaching the stream that crossed a farmer's property, she turned right to make her way up to the old bridge. She was beginning to believe that she was far enough to relax when a dog's urgent bark was followed by a man's shout. Her deepest fears were realized. They had tracked her here. She could not possibly let them find her and especially not with the satchel.

Aria knew the dogs would not be able to track her across the water. She took a deep breath, recalling the need to keep moving forward despite any setbacks. She glanced to her left and saw the tree marked with a subtle "X." It marked the most advantageous crossing point south of the bridge, something her uncle routinely did on his normal paths.

She tested the water's temperature, and the iciness made her shudder. Gritting her teeth as she hiked her skirt up to keep it dry, she steeled herself and made her way across the stream.

Once on the other side, she hid behind a large tree and allowed herself to breathe. She was shivering, but safe. She heard a noise and risked a glance back across the water. She saw at least two dogs and several men. Alexander was one of them, and he was looking right at her. Her legs felt numb, but she didn't dare move. They stood for a long moment, staring at each other while the other men searched the ground.

"There," Alexander said, pointing. But he wasn't pointing at her. He was pointing at the muddy bank. "Her footprints lead north, toward the bridge."

Only after the men started upstream did she rub her hands together and then gently massage her legs.

She wished she had more of her uncle in her and could summon his calm demeanor at will. She wished she could be far away. She allowed herself to close her eyes. Images of her uncle, his laughter, and how it felt when she was small and he swung her high into the air and then onto his shoulders flooded her mind. She smiled to herself and then steeled her resolve for what was ahead. She would not allow herself to wallow in excuses; she would be grateful for every opportunity she had to live out her purpose.

Her mind was pulled back to the present when she heard a faint sound, like a huff. She risked a peek around the tree to scan the brush and made out a flash of silvery gray. Ulrick's horse. He must have circled back. She gritted her teeth, momentarily allowing her internal critic to seize control of her inner thoughts. At least he wasn't on the horse now. If he had been, she'd have seen him. And he'd have seen her.

She glanced to her left and right. Where was he?

With the recognition that she might be discovered any moment, she closed her eyes. A plan. She needed a plan. Her arms almost involuntarily crossed and hugged her shoulders. Her fichu, tied around her neck. Of course! She quickly untied the red ribbon from her hair, unpinned the fichu, and went to work. The moves were second nature to her; so often had she used this during the games with her uncle. Those games, she thought in a flash, were all designed to prepare me. She grabbed a rock from the ground and placed it inside the makeshift slingshot. "Aria, use what you have to do what you need." It was her uncle's voice, echoing inside her mind as if he were right there with her. It gave her comfort even as her heart took off racing.

She knew her distraction would buy her only a few seconds, but that was all she needed.

Like David launching a stone at Goliath's head, Aria swung her right arm back and, in a quick circle, her hand propelled the stone at such a rapid speed that she understood how David killed the enemy giant. It catapulted the stone fast and high, sending it sailing far from her location.

Thump! The rock crashed into the trunk of a wide tree, sending an echo into the air.

As she hoped, Ulrick made a noise and started toward the rock. She now knew where he was. She grabbed the satchel and slipped quietly away from him, using bushes as cover, but still glancing behind to make sure she was undiscovered. She moved quickly and reached Ulrick's horse.

Uncle Raymond had always admired her skill with horses. She reached for the horse and spoke in soft tones. The large horse responded to her gentle touch and voice. In seconds, she was on the horse and riding back toward Robert and Mae's house.

Mae was outside. Aria wasted no time explaining details. She needed to trust her friends, and she needed them to act without hesitation. Mae might not have understood it all, but she comprehended the urgency. "Don't you worry!" Mae said in a tone of determination that engendered confidence. "I will have Robert ride out and send them in the opposite direction. Go!"

Aria smiled and, thanking Mae, jumped off the horse and onto another. She then sent Ulrick's horse running. Anything to confuse and delay.

Aria headed directly for the docks, where she could take passage across the water and buy time. There was nothing here for her now anyway, and she would relish starting over. In the back of her mind, Aria thought about Uncle Raymond and how he also had wanted to start fresh. "I'm taking a part of you with me, my dear uncle," she whispered as she galloped away on his horse.

As Aria neared her destination, she allowed herself to breathe deeply and relax. She dismounted the horse and walked a path in the woods toward the docks. She realized she was now calm. Her heart wasn't beating too crazily; she wasn't perspiring; she was at peace and yet full of adrenaline at the same time. How strange, she thought, that her very mission was at risk and yet she could feel so calm, so free. Despite the urgency of her situation, her thoughts seemed to slow. She realized that it had been worth it. She would do it all over again. She had followed her life's purpose, and she had poured everything she knew into her mission.

Finally, at the docks, she realized she would make it. Aria purchased her ticket. With some time, and with only what she had on her back, she entered a shop to buy supplies that she would need for the journey.

After purchasing some items, Aria waited to board. She wondered what would happen, whether she was doing the right thing. She closed her eyes and pictured her uncle Raymond. He was talking to her with a soothing voice, encouraging her, letting her know that all would be well. She risked a peek into the satchel to make sure the box was there. Silly, she thought, since she could plainly feel its weight. Everything was in order.

Finally, she boarded the ship that would give her passage away from all of this and to a new beginning.

⌘⌘⌘

MISTAKE NINE

The months following David's encounter with the Artist were intense. Pushing himself way out of his comfort zone, David agreed to speak in public. The first opportunity came to him from his mastermind group. He was asked to join a panel discussion at a conference. David was pleased by his performance but was surprised at how well it was received. The next thing he knew, he was invited to be one of the keynote speakers at a conference three weeks later.

There's no way. I am not a speaker. I'm not doing it. No way.

He remembered the thoughts coming, one by one, each like a sharp pin close to a balloon, ready to pop the idea. His new group of friends encouraged him and allayed his concerns. He remembered how a teacher once told him, "You're not a public speaker," and he knew that was a false label. He thought of other excuses and knew he needed to push outside of his comfort zone.

The day finally arrived, and David was standing backstage, his legs were wobbly, his hands trembling. He closed his eyes and felt a warm hand on his shoulder. The Playwright, the actress who taught him the very first mistake, whispered some encouraging words in his ear. He hadn't seen her since she had disappeared that day, and her words of encouragement gave him a shot of confidence.

Not only was he a big success, but his unique presentation style stood out from the rest. Mistake seven had him thinking of ways to stand out, and that he did. Afterward, several individuals approached him to talk about his work. Soon after that, he realized that, instead of another job, he could go directly to his ultimate dream and start his own firm. Sure, there were other firms that would compete, but David knew that he could find a niche of his own. *There's unlimited success available. I will tap into its never-ending supply.* His thoughts were supportive, moving him in the direction of his destiny. That was a far cry from when he started on this journey.

The following Saturday, instead of sleeping in, David was up early.

He glanced down at a scar on his arm from a long-ago bike crash. He traced its line from his elbow down a few inches to his forearm. The thickened skin was barely visible but served as a reminder of the memory, now distant.

It reminded him of his job, once a gaping wound, and then a scab, followed by a slow healing process. His own journey with his employer felt exactly like this and, now, after all of the ups and downs, it felt distant. The struggles with his boss, the worry about his own survival, the rebuilding of his reputation. All in the past, and yet reminders of it stayed with him.

Sometimes he sat and let his mind wander. Had someone seen him, as he sat cross-legged on his sofa, his half-closed eyes staring into the darkness, his breathing as still as an unrippled pond, they would think he was in a trance, perhaps one practiced to achieve a meditative state. It was in these times, half awake, half asleep, that he pondered the mistakes, the lessons, and the wisdom from the Teachers who had crossed his path. Each lesson was interwoven with the next, and he found himself revisiting his life and his decisions. In these moments he contemplated his purpose, his future, and his destiny.

This morning, he was thinking once again about his job. He was finally leaving, and on good terms. He had already put in his three weeks' notice. He was looking forward to his new adventure. And he was ready. Four sizable clients were waiting, and two others had initiated discussions.

Today was one of the last days with his company. He didn't need to do it. Since he was leaving, no one would expect him to comply. Each year, the company sponsored a volunteer day to give back to the community. Employees signed up with various charities and spent the day working alongside others. They would find themselves doing anything from serving meals at a homeless shelter to painting buildings in a dilapidated part of town. David didn't choose. Instead, he allowed the boss to pick for him. "Wherever most needed" was the box he had checked on the form.

Seeing the company choice surprised him. He didn't even realize it was an option. The local hospice. David knew very little about what they did there, but what he did know made him very uncomfortable. Death and dying was something to avoid, not to voluntarily embrace on an otherwise quiet afternoon. He exhaled and thought he would get through it somehow, if only to prove that he had done his duty until the last day of his company service.

He stepped into the street, where an unusually warm breeze for early spring caught him by surprise. The sun's heat already reached through the clouds, hinting of even warmer days ahead.

He walked slowly, dodging a few children who were playing on the sidewalk, and made his way to the hospice. When he reached the address, he looked up at the two large wooden doors. He had probably passed this place hundreds of times and had paid no attention to it. He hadn't realized what it was.

All of a sudden, he felt nervous. He was more uncomfortable with it than he had expected to be.

Steeling himself, David bounded up the steps and pulled the heavy door open. He found himself in a room where a receptionist welcomed him as if they were long-lost brothers. He signed in.

"Aren't you lucky?" said the receptionist in a baritone voice that echoed in the lobby in a way that made David feel like he was auditioning for a radio show. "You're assigned to our very best Doctor."

As if on cue, a tall man entered. He wasn't wearing a white coat, but for some reason, David knew he was the Doctor. His unruly brown hair was losing a war with gray. His brown eyes sparkled as he smiled and shook David's hand like a politician—right hand with a firm grip and left hand grasping his forearm. It was warm, sincere, and it immediately eased David's fears.

"I guess that's me," he said, nodding to the receptionist. "I'm the Doctor. But most people just call me Doc. You must be David."

"Yes, I guess that's me," said David, smiling back. "I'm a bit nervous," he added, almost as an afterthought.

"Don't you worry about a thing," said the Doctor. "By the time you leave, you'll be glad you came."

He scribbled something down on the sign-in pad and then hustled across the lobby. Turning, he said, "David, you're with me today. And you're going to have to keep up!"

He picked up his pace and was gone behind a door. David looked over at the receptionist, who just shrugged his shoulders, nodded, and handed him a visitor badge. David grabbed the plastic badge and clipped it onto his shirt as he crossed the room to find the Doctor.

No sooner did he darken the threshold of the door than he saw the Doctor enter what was obviously a patient room on the left. He went to the door but paused uneasily outside. A voice cut through the still air. "Come on in. I don't bite."

The voice was immediately followed by the Doctor's. "Everyone knows you're visiting today, David. You have several people who are excited to meet you."

"Me?" asked David, his voice traveling up an octave as he expressed his surprise.

David entered the room. It was decorated and designed as if it was a living room, not the hospital-like room he had expected. The Doctor motioned for him to sit down in the chair beside the bed. The man in it turned himself so he could see David. He looked at him and pushed his white hair out of his eyes. The Doctor briefly explained all that the man had endured, all of the surgeries, all of the tests. At that moment, though, it was as if he was free of all of it. "I'm sure glad to have a chance to talk with you."

Not knowing what to say, David decided to remain quiet. He let the silence flow into the room, in between the beeping and whooshing sounds the Doctor's equipment was making as he ran some tests.

"I'm OK with dying," the man said, surprisingly. David knew that hospice meant the inevitable, but he didn't expect to talk about it. In fact, he wanted the entire subject to go away. He was hoping to never speak of it. Maybe he could switch the topic to football or the weather. He was okay with visiting, but he wasn't ready to talk about this.

But the man was intent on talking about his impending death. "I've made my peace. Not only am I filled with faith and sure of where I am going," he said, "but I also have the chance to talk with you. You're young, but you can learn these ideas at any age. One thing you should learn while you can: When you find yourself staring at the abyss called death, you don't care about your bank account. You don't look at the scoreboard. You think about the people you love. You think about your mission on this planet."

David looked over at the man and saw one of the biggest smiles he had ever seen. It seemed to warm the whole room. He looked up at the Doctor, who was fiddling with one of the machines even as he never took his eyes off of his patient.

David took a deep breath. He eased back into the chair and listened. He had never had someone so close to the end talk to him, and it was not what he expected. The man asked about David's life, and the two talked for quite some time. In these moments, the current surroundings disappeared, and they were just two people talking about what really matters in life.

The Doctor was now finished. "Time for you to get some sleep," he said. "And we have others to visit."

The man reached over and grasped David's hand, and David leaned in and gave him a hug. He felt oddly connected after only a short period of time. And, though the man was clearly struggling, obviously in pain, the beautiful smile on his face would have lit up a city block.

As the Doctor and David left the room, David couldn't stop thinking about him.

The Doctor left no room for conversation before they visited another patient, and then another. Both were asleep, but the Doctor asked David to assist in various ways. The fourth was wide awake, sitting on a chair.

His room had a sofa and David, now comfortable in his surroundings, walked right over and sat down and introduced himself. The man was a farmer, but not a simple one. Underneath his calm, quiet demeanor, David could sense a shrewd manager. He imagined that his farm was run with extraordinary discipline.

"To answer your question, it's my heart," he said, answering a question that David didn't even have. "It's finally had enough. Until a major heart attack last year, I somehow thought of myself as your age," he said, "like I was not aging. But look at me. I'm asking myself, 'How did this happen?'"

David just looked back at him, not sure what to say.

"Not the heart attack, of course," the farmer said. "I mean me getting older." He laughed to himself. "Ben Franklin once said, 'Many people die at twenty-five and are buried at seventy-five.'" He laughed even harder. "That's not me. I've had a blast, done everything."

The farmer paused to catch his breath and sip some water before continuing. "Each of us is given so many days to make a difference. We know it, but deep down here,"—the farmer's large hand tapped his chest—"we don't seem to believe it. Now I do. I finally understand. I'm so grateful, so thankful. I've had an amazing life. I just want to spend my remaining days telling everyone to be thankful for every single day."

With that, the two began a conversation that ran the gamut from life to sports to business.

David didn't even realize that the Doctor had left the room until he was back in the doorway. The two had talked so naturally that he didn't know how much time had passed. David leaned in and hugged the farmer, felt his tough skin on his face, and squeezed his muscular shoulder. David promised he would return again another day.

The Doctor then led David down the hallway, up some stairs, and into what was obviously his office. "The patients here seem so...I don't know...calm, peaceful. I'm surprised," David said, lost in thought.

The Doctor nodded and poured them both some iced tea. He listened as David shared his observations of the people he had met at the hospice.

Shifting in his seat, the Doctor said, "I've learned such incredible lessons on living from those who are dying. I've learned that life is precious. Every morning the gift of time appears. Wrapped in the day's worries, many miss its power. We must push the worries aside and enjoy the present. Whether or not you will fulfill your purpose depends on what you do with the present."

The Doctor stood up, walked over to a shelf, and picked up a familiar leather-bound book. It was worn and fit into his hands like it was part of him.

"You, too?" David asked. "Does *everyone* own a copy of that book?"

The Doctor grinned. "Actually there are only ten known copies. It's the gift that changed everything for me. I learned each of the mistakes, studied them, and worked like mad not to fall into them. The last one, for me, that one really hit me only after I started working here."

"What's the last one?" David inquired. "I'm dying to know." As soon as he said it, realizing where he was, he wished he could retract the words.

But the Doctor just laughed, more comfortable with dying than David ever felt he could be. "Mistake number nine is believing you have all the time in the world."

David nodded, and now he realized why he was here. The mystery of it all was inexplicable, but the order and timing was something he now appreciated. David helped himself to some more iced tea from a pitcher on the table.

The Doctor's gaze was intensely focused on David. "It's difficult to think of our own mortality. Living each day for its intended purpose. I've learned that it's important to think about both of those things: on the one hand, live each day as if it's your last and, on the other, as if it's your first. Your last keeps you focused on what really matters. You think about people, about loving those around you. Your first is important because you also must have a longer view, or you will never accomplish the goals that are hard and take longer.

"My confession: I have been better at thinking I am at the beginning than at the end. But, knowing there is an end, which working here has made me realize, wow, has that ever crystalized my thinking about what really matters. I am thinking about my purpose in a whole new light!"

David found himself nodding and nodding—so much so that he tried to stop himself but then found himself doing it again.

"If we realize that time is limited, we still have a great time, still do the fun things, but we also feel a sense of urgency. That drive is what distinguishes successful people from the ordinary. Do you want to be average? If so, then take all the time you need!

"When we realize the value of time, we respect it. We are more often on time for meetings because we don't want to waste someone else's time. Time demands respect."

The Doctor glanced at David, who was paying rapt attention. So he continued. "But here's what is equally powerful. A sense of urgency is good, but a frenetic pace can cause mistakes. Some decisions benefit from immediate action. Other decisions are best made with reflection. Why? Because time seasons, it matures, it flavors, it weaves ideas and layers of creativity with each hour."

"How do you know when to move fast and when to give yourself more time?" David asked, genuinely confused.

"That takes time," the Doctor said, laughing at the irony as he said it. "Seriously, that is wisdom. Wisdom teaches when to act and when not to. When I was younger, I would act immediately, and then I learned to slow some things down."

David and the Doctor talked about time, about impact, about making a difference. From the beginning of this process, David had moved from uncomfortable to expectant. He no longer shied away from the lessons but was asking questions, trying to understand more, not only about the concepts but also about the experiences. He realized that each one of the mistakes was now a part of his thinking.

"A beautiful life is one played on the strings of our purpose. Our time may be limited, but our impact continues beyond us through love. Giving time to others is the most precious opportunity to leave a lasting impact. The first mistake is about purpose because your purpose is the compass, pointing the way for a good use of time. Without it, you have no sense of direction."

David needed to stretch, and so he walked over to the window and glanced up and down the street. The street was unusually quiet. He loved the old architecture of this part of the city. He noticed an old phone booth on the corner, a throwback to an earlier time that somehow looked just right. A shopkeeper was tidying up the front of her store.

As he was gazing out the window, David felt a familiar tingle at the back of his neck. He felt it when someone was watching him. He turned and saw a pretty girl in the doorway. "Oh, you already have a visitor," she said. "Should I come back later?"

David suddenly realized who it was. It was her! The young woman who had started this incredible journey when her papers were blown into the wind. His mouth dropped open before he covered it with his hand.

"Aria, I want you to meet David," the Doctor said. "You two have a lot to talk about. You've both been on the same journey."

"I wondered," Aria said, a twinkle in her eye. "I thought I saw you outside the bookstore not too long ago."

David composed himself. "I want to say, 'It's nice to meet you,' but I guess we've already met. Your name...Aria...did the Bartender tell you that was the name of his bar back when it was an inn?"

"Actually, it was owned by one of my ancestors. The name has been in my family for a few hundred years," she replied.

The Doctor cast a knowing look their way and said, "Would you two excuse me? I'm sorry, Aria, but I need to see you later. Maybe the two of you could go get a bite to eat together and compare notes. I'm sure you have a lot in common." He wasn't subtle about his wink. Aria's skin immediately turned a few shades darker.

"Would you join me? It would be my pleasure." David was smiling and looking directly into her eyes with hope.

"I'd be happy to," she answered.

David thanked the Doctor for the day together and promised to return. He wanted to visit his new friends again and meet the others he had missed.

David and Aria found their way out of the hospital. David noticed he walked with a bounce that he didn't have when he arrived. Stepping outside, he instinctively reached into his coat pocket to ensure the paper was there. Just as he suspected, it was.

He now knew the nine mistakes. He knew all of them. And he had finally found her. He silently repeated her name over and over, like a melody playing in his mind.

As the two of them walked through town, they found the conversation natural and comfortable. They had so much to discuss.

Later that evening, as David returned home, he marveled at his journey. He decided he was going to double down and make sure he lived in a way that would take full advantage of the wisdom in the lessons. He fished the paper out of his pocket and read the words.

MISTAKE #9:
Believing You Have All the Time in the World

Time is a gift wrapped in the day's worries. Push the worries aside and enjoy the present.

Whether you will fulfill your purpose depends on what you do with the present.

Live each day as if it is your first and your last.

Knowing your life is limited will keep you focused on the most important part of your purpose.

Successful people have a sense of urgency.

Some decisions require the maturity of time, which delicately weaves ideas and insight with each hour.

A beautiful life is one played on the strings of our purpose.

Love continues our impact long past our time.

Your purpose is the compass pointing the way for you to use time wisely.

THE THIRD LAW

⌘⌘⌘

Aria stared at the marker she had commissioned to remember her uncle Raymond. The summer sun, warming her back, cast a shadow across its face. She read her uncle's name and the dates carved into the stone, a stark reminder of the reality of his death. She often visited here and talked with him in the quiet gardens. She updated him even in death as she always had in life. She admired the local stonecutter's work, the way he integrated the design. She read the quoted inscription on the bottom and laughed at its irony. "For the Lord God does nothing without revealing his secret to his servants the prophets" (Amos 3:7).

Her uncle certainly had many secrets, and now she did, too. She brushed some loose dirt off the stone. Memories of him flooded her mind, and she smiled. His impact on her life was extraordinary.

Today she found herself telling her uncle about the man she had married, about their children, and about the Teachers. In fact, she had gotten to really know her future husband when she chose him as one of the nine teachers. She had come to tell her uncle about him the day she decided he would be one of the Nine. It was healing for her to do this, kept him close somehow.

"Uncle Raymond, you, of all people, know this, but I've found the best teachers often are the ones who made the mistakes they now teach. My husband knows the importance of surrounding yourself with the right people."

At that moment, a long shadow danced across her own in the grass. She turned and squinted in the sun.

It was him. Alexander.

He smiled that crooked smile of his, and she reached out and took his hand. His journey, his mistakes, his pursuit of the truth, and then finally of her, all of it was part of their story together.

Aria marveled at it all. From inheriting her uncle's role as Keeper to her marriage, she didn't quite understand everything, but she dutifully fulfilled her part. She longed for the day when the book and the laws would be available to all of humanity.

She whispered a farewell to her uncle, and together she and Alexander stepped onto the well-worn path and made their way back home. She felt so alive. Whenever she was acting within her purpose, her energy soared. The two of them ran a local inn outside of Philadelphia. They enjoyed teaching the mistakes and wondered what impact the Book would have on the colonies.

Back at home, Aria removed the Book from its hiding place. She read it often. This evening, she read the Third Law of the Keeper. It was only a few short sentences, but its message was something she needed to read over and over again. How many times had she read these lessons? Easily hundreds of times.

Only the Keeper of the Nine would ever read this page until

everything was revealed to the world. It had been this way for generations of Keepers.

She wondered who had written it and how long ago.

She read it again to herself in a whisper:

The Law of Belief

The Law of Belief is the third and final law. The Almighty created you with purpose. Believe in yourself. What seems impossible and implausible is only the enemy of your potential.

Develop an unshakeable, unwavering, unbendable faith in your ability. Your destiny will expand as your belief expands. There are really no limits to what is possible for you.

Allow your beliefs to soar like an eagle. You cannot rise higher than your own beliefs. Most importantly, when you are able, help instill belief in others. This is the most important task of all—for once belief multiplies, nothing shall be impossible.

Aria realized that she saw something new in this message every time she read it.

The message was powerful.

She turned the page over and read the notations meant for the Keeper: how to choose the Nine, especially finding candidates who exhibited the Three Laws of the Keeper; how each Keeper must move to a new geographic location and find teachers; and how the Nine may think that they have the only copies, but that there were others, just like them, in various parts of the world, spreading the message. How many of them there were, she couldn't say. She knew there were many mysteries about it all that would elude her in this lifetime.

Aria wondered about the Three Laws of the Keeper and how they powered a true leader in ways that she continued to study.

She tucked the final page back into the manuscript and looked out the window. It was time for her to select the next student of the mistakes, though she realized that in some ways, she was never the one really selecting. It was part of the mystery that moved people and events into place. She called it providence. Still, she enjoyed the opportunity to share *The Book of Mistakes* with willing students of its powerful message.

⌘⌘⌘

EPILOGUE

It was a Saturday morning, and David woke up early. Though he had wanted to sleep in, at his first stirring, his mind flooded him with thoughts, each one harnessing his attention until forming an unbreakable bond, shaking him from sleep and pulling him into consciousness.

Unlike waking under the stress of work or fear or negativity, as he once had, he woke these days with the pull of his purpose. His dreams, his hopes, they infused him with an unstoppable energy and motion. Often he felt that his dream was the train engine, and he was in the caboose, going along for the ride.

The labels others sought to brand on him no longer limited him. On occasion, he would realize his acceptance of someone else's dream or someone else's definition or his own excuses, and he would allow the power of his thoughts to clear away these invisible strings tying him to a life of less. He no longer allowed others to have power over his destiny.

His friends, at least the ones he spent the most time with, were positive and encouraging. Each friend was like a single, perfectly pitched note. When combined, they provided a rich music to his soul. His friends were truly gifts, and he was so grateful. His best friend was his wife, who was, he could safely say, part of his destiny. With Aria by his side, he felt complete, able to become the man he wanted to be.

On this particular Saturday morning, up before the sun, his thoughts were back on when he first saw her in the park, grabbing at papers. How ironic that she was on the same but parallel journey, and somehow their experiences intertwined. She was not at the first appointment with the Old Man all those years ago, but she had discovered the mistakes on her own path.

How that happened was a mystery they would contemplate but never fully understand.

He walked into his study, an office lined with books, filled with his papers. A fireplace was on the far side of the room, and he built a small fire to warm the room before reaching for a worn leather book.

It was *The Book of Mistakes*, the book that held the wisdom of past experience. The Old Man had willed his copy to the couple with only one condition: they must work to spread its wisdom to those who were seeking it. As the Keeper of the mistakes, he was always in motion. He was always teaching and working to ensure the book's wisdom would endure.

As he crossed the room to settle in his favorite chair, David caught a glimpse of himself in the mirror. No longer could he be called a young man. The gray sprinkled in his hair, the wrinkles from a life of smiles. He sat down, caressing the book, his mind drifting. He glanced up at one of the Artist's paintings on the wall. Though they had moved in their new role as Keepers to seek out nine new Teachers, she remained one of their closest friends.

As he opened the book, a letter from the Old Man dropped into his lap. The words written could have been spoken, because he could hear them as if the Old Man were in the room talking directly to him.

He recalled the first line of the letter. It was one the Old Man shared with him on his second visit to that café only months after he learned the final mistake.

"Live a life that matters, a life of light and of love and of hope. Your choices can either become the wings of your success or the bars that imprison you in a life of mediocrity."

Leaning back into his chair, he read those words again with the confidence and assurance that he was doing just that. He reached into his pocket and felt the coins once given to him by a banker who taught him that his value was not determined by others. He had carried them with him ever since that day; never once had they left his possession.

As he sat there in his chair, he smiled knowingly, already thinking ahead to his breakfast meeting with the newly selected individual who would be next in a long line of people he had taught the mistakes. It was part of his life's work, part of his promise to the Old Man, and part of his purpose.

Your choices can become the wings of success or the bars imprisoning you in a life of mediocrity.

Allow your positive thoughts to clear the invisible strings tying you to a life of less.

Live a life that matters, a life of light and love and hope.

The 9 Secrets to Creating a Successful Future

1. Live your own dream.
2. Recognize your inherent value.
3. Reject excuses.
4. Surround yourself with the right people.
5. Explore outside your comfort zone.
6. Move forward through challenges with determination and purpose.
7. Stand out.
8. Act boldly with the knowledge that your potential for success is unlimited.
9. Pursue your goals with urgency.

ACKNOWLEDGMENTS

Over twenty-five years ago, my beautiful wife became my greatest cheerleader. I am so grateful to share life with you. Thank you, Anita, for all you do for our family and how you model the pursuit of truth.

Thank you to my daughter, Joy, who read every draft of this manuscript and talked about ideas and characters. No one will celebrate more than I when you start releasing your own books.

My mom, dad, sisters, and brother for your incredible love and influence in my life. What an incredibly unique family experience we enjoyed, allowing us to learn from others while impacting the world.

Thank you to Rolf Zettersten, who was my friend long before he was my publisher, and who has been an encouraging voice since the day I met him. I'm appreciative of the team at Center Street, especially my editor, Christina Boys, who guided this first-time author through numerous drafts. Thanks also to Patsy Jones, Katie Connors, Katie Broaddus, and the many others across Hachette Book Group who helped make this book a reality.

I'm grateful for my agent, Shannon Marven, and her wonderful team at Dupree Miller, who are the best in the business.

Thank you to Steve Pate, who read the earliest versions and not only provided feedback, but encouraged me to publish it.

Whether through books, seminars, or deep conversations, I'm the beneficiary of many people's counsel and have poured that learning into these pages. I won't even begin to list them all, because the book would double in size. God has filled my life with people who encourage and challenge so that I may fulfill my dreams.

Finally, thank you for reading this book and sharing its message with others.

ABOUT THE AUTHOR

SKIP PRICHARD is an accomplished global CEO, growth-oriented business leader, and keynote speaker. He is known for his track record of successfully repositioning companies and dramatically improving results. Listed as a top 100 leadership speaker by *Inc.* magazine, he is a regular keynote speaker on topics ranging from leadership and personal development to corporate turnarounds and culture change. *Harvard Business Review* labeled him a "relentless giver" and a "standout example" of a social CEO. His *Leadership Insights* blog has received numerous awards and he has interviewed hundreds of leaders from Secretary of State Condoleezza Rice to journalist Dan Rather to baseball great John Smoltz. His views have been featured in print and broadcast media including the BBC, the *New York Times*, CNN, NPR, the *Daily Beast*, *Harvard Business Review*, *Information Today*, the *Bookseller*, *Publishers Weekly*, *Christian Retailing*, and the *Library Journal*. He lives in Ohio and Tennessee with his wife, Anita, and daughter, Joy. Connect with the author at skipprichard.com.